INKLINGS
On Philosophy & Theology

By Matthew Dominguez

Conversations on
the Trust Lists

A new way of learning about our
connections with truth and reality
Inklings: On Philosophy & Theology

By Matthew Dominguez

First printing September 2000
Fifteenth printing May 2015

Scripture quotations marked (NIV) are taken from the Holy Bible, New International Version®, NIV®. Copyright © 1973, 1978, 1984, 2011 by Biblica, Inc.™ Used by permission of Zondervan. All rights reserved worldwide. www.zondervan.com The "NIV" and "New International Version" are trademarks registered in the United States Patent and Trademark Office by Biblica, Inc.™

Scripture quotations marked ESV are from The Holy Bible, English Standard Version® (ESV®), copyright © 2001 by Crossway, a publishing ministry of Good News Publishers. Used by permission. All rights reserved.

Scripture quotations marked NASB are taken from the New American Standard Bible®, Copyright © 1960, 1962, 1963, 1968, 1971, 1972, 1973, 1975, 1977, 1995 by The Lockman Foundation
Used by permission." (www.Lockman.org)

ISBN-13: 978-0692229934 (WheatonPress.com)
ISBN-10: 0692229930

This title available at Amazon.com or wherever fine books are sold. Please visit the publisher online at www.WheatonPress.com for more books in this series, classroom or small group discounts, and other resources designed to equip you in your discipleship journey.

Dedication

For my students, a thousand thanks.

And to Batman – you are a true hero.
(You know who you are. Thanks again.)

I trust you will find the information on these pages helpful
On your journey
As you peruse the bits of material dappled here and there
It is important to keep in mind
The daily decisions we make in life
Are based on our conclusions concerning the nature of Reality.

Everyone is trusting.
The only way we live
Eat, sleep, move, communicate, eke out an existence
Is to make decisions based on whatever we consider
Trustworthy.

As long as humans have engaged in conversation
And shared ideas,
We have differed on the object of

Our trust,
Our faith,
Our belief,
Our confidence.

Most philosophers agree that Plato and Aristotle's works on
The True Nature of Reality
Are a foundation for all human interaction;

And although epic cultural shifts have ensued…
Races and religions have been defined…
Empires have risen and fallen…

Every individual continues to make every single decision
Based on whom and what he or she trusts
As true,
As real,

As *worthy*
of trust.

CONTENTS

"And you will know the [T]ruth,
and the [T]ruth will set you free."

John 8:32 (ESV)

The Mind is everything.
What you think you become.

Buddha

Do not be conformed to this world,
but be transformed by the renewal of your mind,
that by testing you may discern what is the will of God,
what is good and acceptable and perfect.

The Apostle Paul
Romans 12:2 (ESV)

INTRODUCTION

"The birth of Christ is the eucatastrophe of man's history. The resurrection is the eucatastrophe of the story of the incarnation. This story begins and ends in Joy! It has pre-eminently the 'inner consistence of reality.' There is no tale ever told that men would rather find as true, and none which so many skeptical men have accepted as true on its own merits."

> J.R.R. Tolkien
> "On Fairy Stories"
> from *Leaf and Tree*[1]

We all have to pick a story to make sense of our world. The story you currently and ultimately choose to trust is how you will frame your day-to-day reality. Erwin McManus, an influential, insightful pastor in California, says that in our competitive, media-packed modern culture, "The best story wins." I think this has been true for humanity ever since the invention of language and story time around a warm, intimate fire under the innumerable twinkling, smiling, listening stars.

Over the past twenty years, what I have found to be trustworthy and true, especially when it comes to making sense of our world and of reality, is that we all live a life of faith. Furthermore, as we faithfully trust various stories, transmitted generation to generation, creatively invented or adapted, unconsciously consumed or intentionally adopted as our own, we often forget that these tales are human attempts to explain the inexplicable and to comprehend the incomprehensible. More importantly, we often forget (or deny) that all of these stories are theories. They are our best attempts to get it right. They are the distilled essence of our collective efforts to describe what is Really Real and what is Truly True. We all want to know what is really going on in the universe.

My approach to worldview, and thus, philosophy, is simple and practical. It builds off of and extends the iconic works on the nature and consequences of our beliefs on Prime Reality generated by Socrates, Plato, and Aristotle. In essence, these brilliant minds helped us clearly see that the spiritual (the immaterial) and the material are the two basic ingredients for the fabric of reality. From this foundation I propose that there are four basic story lines available to humanity.

- Idealism is the belief that only the spiritual immaterial world is real.

- Materialism trusts in the reality of only the measurable realm of matter.

- Monism believes in the unified existence of the spiritual and material realm as one gigantic entity.

- Theism embraces the reality of both the spiritual realm and the material realm but maintains an understanding of real unity and real distinction between the two.

Studying these four main options in conjunction with several of the essential questions of life, and understanding the consequences of trusting the various answers these questions generate brings clarity and awareness. As we learn, we are empowered to make intelligent and informed choices on the multitude of religions and "isms" available to each human.

With this in mind, this book lends itself to be broken into different scenes in a personal story. In acts one, two, and three I offer the reader a philosophical approach to studying worldview through defining these four main options for interpreting reality. The four worldviews are set up as four distinct "trust lists." It is essential for all people to have the freedom and dignity to make their own choices about their personal beliefs. I want to intentionally create a safe and healthy forum for exploration, discovery, and authentic self discovery. I want people to have a greater sense of awareness and ownership for not only what they choose to believe, but also why they believe what they believe in the context of so many options. I tell my students all the time that I have no desire to create a weak and insufficient or biased description of a certain worldview to sway opinion or manipulate their decisions. Please keep in mind that this text is intentionally not a text on religions or a laundry list of "isms". There are already plenty of those on bookshelves and online; rather, this text offers a new way of thinking critically about what we trust and why we trust what we trust. The lens of philosophy can empower you to understand what you and others believe through the lens of philosophy. The lens of philosophy also makes it possible for you to be able to learn more about the particulars of beliefs in the context of other beliefs.

However, it is also important to note that acts four and five of this text are my overt, unashamed attempt to invite any reader or student to learn more about my understanding of Christ as the fullness of reality. The story I choose to believe as the True Story is the unfolding drama of one that I believe we are all in; it has Christ's birth, life, death, resurrection, and commissioning as the centerpiece and the main plot of the entire story of human existence. I believe that all great stories point towards and invite us into greater participation in the

Greatest Story. Therefore, the last acts of this book specifically speak to those who want to learn more of what it means to be a Christ follower or who are interested in what authentic Christ followers believe. If you are not interested in trusting in Christ at this moment on your journey, I hope you will be able to read this book in a way where you can see why other people do choose to trust in Him. Either way, this book should clarify your understanding of the major worldviews available to humans while simultaneously offering an invitation to a fresh perspective of the Grace and Truth found in the person of Jesus.

The writings and stories of G.K. Chesterton, C.S. Lewis, and J.R.R. Tolkien mindfully encourage a cogent, intelligent, and reasonable approach to start or to continue trusting in the Story of Christ, let alone the Person of Christ. One of their favorite things to do was have hearty conversations on the topics in these pages, usually in a pub over a meal seasoned with deep laughter. I also encourage anyone to get to know the unique journeys each of these brilliant minds and hearts experienced in their pursuit of the Truth. It is the main reason why act five of this text is all about conversation and personal Journey.

G.K. Chesterton devoured, digested, and had the ability to retain the information in thousands of books on his unflinching, unquenchable quest for the Truth. Ultimately, a personal relationship with Jesus Christ was the best option his massive heart and mind were able to find as truly satisfying and fulfilling. J.R.R. Tolkien's *Hobbit* and *Lord of the Rings* are written as powerful, mythical, metaphoric, epic, adventure, fantasy stories that are intentionally designed to point us to our role in the powerful, real life, mythical, epic, adventure, fantasy story that we are in. He reminds us that the book of Acts in the Bible does not say "the end" when we finish chapter twenty-eight. C.S. Lewis grew up as a Christian, then became an devout atheist for over two decades, and then chose to fully commit to the Christian Story as the True Story, the "True Myth," as he calls it. He says this about the Story of Christ in his essay "The Myth Became Fact," "The myth became flesh. This is not a religion nor a philosophy; it's the summing up and actuality of them all. For this is the marriage of heaven and earth: perfect Myth and perfect Fact; claiming not only our love and obedience, but also our wonder and delight addressed to the savage, the child, and the poet in each one of us no less then to the moralist, the scholar, and the philosopher."[2]

Please keep in mind as I mix and match the metaphors in this book and my class that I assume an essential truth: the metaphors are not reality. No metaphor is or can be; Christ is. I invite students and readers to go beyond metaphor, theology, religion, trust lists, and worldviews into a relationship with a living being, with the Living, Loving Being Himself, Jesus Christ. Because I am also a lover and teacher of literature, this book is organized in acts following a plot line of sorts and finishing with a climax. This is an unfolding story with you, the students and readers, as characters on a continuing journey of discovery and invitation.

The four main trust lists are a picture of how we so often take a piece of Prime Reality and work hard to make that piece into our own version of what we want to be the fullness of reality. The main goal of act four is to describe some of the process of how the life and work of Christ through the Holy Spirit takes the four separate lists, or stories, and knits them back together with Grace and Truth into an inviting relationship with the living, breathing fullness of Reality— Himself.

Thus, it is important for my students and readers to understand from the start that philosophy is a tool like a map. It is a means to an end, and that end is Christ. If this book can help point anyone towards an authentic, life-giving relationship with the person of Christ, it has done its work. Furthermore, through approaching the study of philosophy with dignity and honor, I hope to you find freedom to digest the ideas in this book, feel nourished in the process, and be empowered and free to grow in understanding your worldview, other worldviews, your personal trust list, whether or not Christ is currently an integral part of your story.

Ultimately, this book will do a disservice if it simply gives you more information about reality and philosophy but doesn't point you to the person of Christ. I have no desire at all to make people more "religious" in the traditional sense of the word. Nor do I have any desire to simply create just another traditional book on philosophy or theology. The professional philosophers, theologians, and apologists have provided excellent sources for digging into specific topics of philosophy, doctrine, and theology. I am a teacher and a father and fellow pilgrim who is offering a practical and useful way to organize the massive amounts of information, questions, and answers we are bombarded with on this adventure. These pages are designed to help you have informed consent and greater access to the consequences of the important choices we make concerning belief and trust as connected to everyday living. This book is about the Truth setting you and me free. And this book is about an invitation to seeing the Truth as a Being to be trusted, not just a list of potent statements or axioms. I hope that the pages in this book can help students and readers grow in understanding of the powerful invitation Jesus makes when He claims in the Gospel of John in chapter fourteen verse six that He is, "the [W]ay the [T]ruth and the [L]ife." He, Himself, is the Truth, not a book, or a philosophy, or a world view, or a verse, or a trust list.

Furthermore, in a venue such as this, a short book, I can only hope to introduce you to your own trust list in the context of the other major stories and trust lists. I hope to introduce you to the Master of the House. But you are the one who will need to surrender to His Spirit and to get to know Him personally. I hope to show you truths that can break down walls, open locked doors, expose lies or fears, and invite you into joy, freedom, and love. But please remember that I am only a teacher. And readers and students need to know that I am an adopted Son of my Heavenly Father, Jesus the King of the Universe. Building His Kingdom is what I do, and more importantly it is what I believe and Trust to be true. Do me the honor of learning whatever you can from this information and then continuing on your journey and your quest for Truth.

This book is not nor will it be able to give you The Truth (with a capitol "T"); it is simply a mirror for discovering your own object of trust and a treasure map that will help you find and grow in relationship with the Truth, whom you can trust with full confidence. To paraphrase the apostle John, "You shall know the [Reality] [T]ruth, and that shall make you free." My ultimate hope is that this book brings you closer to the living, resurrected person of Christ—who can and will transform your life.

John muses on this approach to understanding Prime Reality in the first chapter of his gospel (ESV) as he poetically explains and invites us into the True Story:

> In the beginning was the Word, and the Word was with God, and the Word was God. He was in the beginning with God. All things were made through him, and without him was not any thing made that was made. In him was life, and the life was the light of men. The light shines in the darkness, and the darkness has not overcome it.
>
> There was a man sent from God, whose name was John. He came as a witness, to bear witness about the light, that all might believe through him. He was not the light, but came to bear witness about the light.

The true light, which gives light to everyone, was coming into the world. He was in the world, and the world was made through him, yet the world did not know him.

He came to his own, and his own people did not receive him. But to all who did receive him, who believed in his name, he gave the right to become children of God, who were born, not of blood nor of the will of the flesh nor of the will of man, but of God.

And the Word became flesh and dwelt among us, and we have seen his glory, glory as of the only Son from the Father, full of grace and truth.

(John bore witness about him, and cried out, "This was he of whom I said, 'He who comes after me ranks before me, because he was before me.'") For from his fullness we have all received, grace upon grace.

For the law was given through Moses; [G]race and [T]ruth came through Jesus Christ..

Reflection

1. What ideas or images stood out to you in this introduction?

2. What was refreshing? Why?

3. What was frustrating? Why?

4. What questions do you have?

ACT I

TRUST:

LIFE ON
FAITH ISLAND

ACT I, SCENE 1

CREATED TO TRUST

Everyone trusts. The only way humans live, eat, sleep, move, communicate, and eke out an existence is to make decisions based on whatever we consider trustworthy. However, as long as humans have enjoyed conversations and shared ideas, we have differed on the object of our trust, our faith, our beliefs, on where we put our confidence.

Although epic cultural shifts have ensued, races and religions have been defined, and empires have risen and fallen, individuals continue to make decisions based on whom and what he or she trusts as true, as really real, as worthy of trust.

We give authority to whom and what we trust.

The more we trust something or someone the more authority we give.

Consciously and subconsciously, whatever we give authority to or have given authority to in the past directly and indirectly influences our current thoughts and behavior.

Ultimately, we each develop personal lists of what we deem to be worthy of our trust. These personal trust lists become the primary influence for how we view and interact with the world.

Unfortunately, not everything to which we give authority is worthy of our trust. Furthermore, we often find ourselves in situations where others assert their authority over us even though we do not trust them. This type of authority often uses fear, inflicts pain, devises external motivators, and exploits ignorance to influence behavior. My teenage nephew Owen poignantly pointed out to me that it often takes great courage to address the issues of trust and trustworthiness, particularly when it comes to changing what we put our trust in or finding freedom from unhealthy, unwanted situations of imposed authority. This is a great place to start our story. This is a story of courage and freedom. Facing the truth about trust and authority and potentially changing the motivation or object of our trust could possibly be the most courageous thing any of us will do. For some of us, standing firm in what we trust to be the truth and what we have found to be genuinely trustworthy in the face of opposition will take similar courage. This is where the adventure begins and, ironically, ends: Trust and Courage.

ACT I, SCENE 2

TRUST LISTS:
A NEW CONCEPT
AND A NEW TOOL

Your worldview is your view both of the world and for the world. You may not live what you profess, but you live what you believe. It's inescapable. We are great at professing, but how we live is rooted in our beliefs. Our worldview is not just a mindset it is a "will set." It's how we live our lives, how we choose our priorities, how we adopt preferences.

A person's worldview is determined by asking the ultimate questions about origin, meaning, morality, and destiny. The answers touch every molecule of the universe—including you. The questions are ultimate because there are answers."

William E. Brown[1]

From a philosophical and even a theological perspective, what I call the four Trust Lists represent the foundations of how we view reality all around us. These four lists, which I mentioned in the introduction and will describe in greater detail later, are idealism, materialism, monism, and theism. They are the catalysts for the substance that forms our core beliefs by providing authentic answers to some of the biggest questions of life. These answers also provide the substance of our shared "isms," religions, and ways. The nature and outcomes of the daily, continuous decisions made by people can be traced, either consciously or subconsciously, to this personal list of what one trusts. As we develop a personal trust list, we intentionally or unintentionally pull from these lists or from an amalgamation of these four lists.

Unfortunately, a large percentage of people are unaware of their own trust list as well as the consequences of trusting certain answers to the big questions they have. Additionally, many people do not realize how much they are influenced by those around them. We come in contact with numerous people each day in our personal lives and in our communities. We are affected by other people's trust lists, because actions, choices, and conversations are based on what an individual chooses to trust. Taken collectively as a larger group, trends in actions, choices, and conversations of groups shapes cultural identity. Many people are unaware of how profoundly they are swayed by the broader macro-culture of which they are a part. Consequently, miscommunication, misunderstandings, friction, and tensions ensue in local and global communities as well as in our own homes.

There are great advantages in identifying our own personal lists of what we deem worthy of our trust and, on a larger scale, the lists of those with whom we share community. Furthermore, increased awareness of where we place our trust opens the door for the creation of personal self awareness while also developing shared awareness. Consequently, we create the opportunity for healthy dialogue and the possibility of shared understanding with others.

For example, consider a conversation I had with my insightful, intuitive daughter, Anna, when she was five years old. Our beloved yellow lab, Pup, died. One of the first questions she asked was, "Papa, where did Pup go?" I could have casually tossed out an answer to satisfy Anna's inquisitiveness. However, there was potentially a powerful subtext to Ann's question. While she was asking what happens when our dog dies, she was also asking what will happen when she dies, when grandpa dies, when her papa dies. Since she trusts me, and because I am her father, she has given massive authority to my answers to her questions. The answer I gave her in that moment influences how she frames the weighty issue of life and death in her unfolding individual story and as a growing member of our immediate community.

The issue at stake is that there are different answers to this question with very different consequences. In his famous "To be or not to be" speech in act three, scene 1 of Shakespeare's play, Prince Hamlet famously ponders the dilemma of "the undiscovered country, from whose bourn no traveler returns." All humans are faced with the inevitability of death, and thus we are forced to deal with the potential options of what actually happens after we die. Interestingly, how we answer that question will directly affect the way we approach the daily moments of our life.

This is where the concept of the trust list works well as a tool to navigate this important scenario and others like it. For example, if I were to approach the situation like an idealist, I would tell Anna that Pup's physical suffering is over and the perfected components of Pup's spirit have been united with the ideal, one, eternal state of spiritual perfection that exists beyond the broken lifeless material body on the floor. Pup has ceased to exist but glimpses and moments of joy, love, and beauty we saw in Pup's snuggles, wags, licks, and walks will live on because they found their source in the spiritual, eternal ideals of goodness, truth, and beauty that exist beyond this finite, incomplete world filled with death, pain, and decay. As Anna continues to grow with that in mind, she might seek solidarity on her journey in connection with the stories found in Buddhism, much of Hinduism, and other religions or "ways" that pull from idealism.

On the other hand, I were to approach the situation as an authentic materialist, I would tell Anna that Pup lived her life as well as she could and it is now done, that her broken body does not have the ability to conduct the electrical impulses needed for reacting to her environment. Anything that we would call "alive" has this end. We were fortunate to be a part of her existence as she was to be part of ours. Pup's well-lived life full of joy, love, and adventure is now done, and we will dispose of her body before it starts to decay, just like we recycle or dispose of a broken electronic toy that cannot be fixed. As Anna grows, she might endeavor to find support to navigate the nuances of life and death in authors such a Nietzsche, Sartre, Camus, Dawkins, and Hitchens.

Alternatively, I could play the opening scene of *The Lion King™* for Anna, and approach this hard but hopeful aspect of Pup's journey like a complete monist. I would mention to Anna that life and death are a natural part of existing in and as a part of the universe. Pup is simply participating in the grand unfolding of the process and life and transformation that all of existence goes through. The energy of life flows in and out of all living things, and Pup is connected to this life force. Her body was born and grew and lived and recently started the process of transformation into another form of existence through decay and dissolution. It is the unfolding exciting adventure of participating in existence and transformation. Like a little larvae growing into a caterpillar, then turning into a butterfly, but then nourishing a baby bird and on and on. Some call this the circle of life. It will happen to all of us, and has been happening forever. If she trusts this to be true Anna might look to Taoism and Theosophy or possibly identify with the perspectives in the New Age movement. Finally, I could talk about how God is a powerful, creative being who created animals and humans. I could tell her a story like the one about Adam and Eve and all of the animals in a loving, perfect relationship with their Creator and with each other. This would give some context to talking with Anna about how this creative God has power over life and death and eternal life for all His creation and creatures. I could help her understand that I do not know exactly what has happened to "Pup" because none of us are God. He has not been overtly specific and concrete about what He does with animals when they die. Therefore, God has intentionally put us in a position to trust Him as a powerful, loving being with what will happen to Pup now that her body has suffered the consequences of being a part of this world. I could talk to her about God's eternal Kingdom where no one will die anymore. As she grows, Anna might gravitate towards the theistic religions, their leaders, and their texts to make sense of the complexities of life and death.

These are four very different answers with vastly different consequences and potentially polarizing outcomes. It also serves to highlight the important truth that the questions in life, particularly from a five-year-old, force us to use what we trust to develop responses to the daily unfolding circumstances and queries naturally all around. It also serves to show how this moment could powerfully influence the direction Anna takes as she continues on her journey of choosing what she believes. I know that my response may not have much influence at all, but it could.

I used what I trusted to craft the best response for my daughter in that moment. As a philosophy teacher, I had a vast number of options to pull from to help shape her perspective of reality and help develop her own, personal understanding of the story of her life in the context of Pup's death. Anna accessed the perspective of someone she trusted. She willingly gave me authority in her life to help her make sense of the lifeless body of her furry friend in front of the fireplace on the floor of our living room.

ACT I, SCENE 3

FAITH & FAITH ISLAND

We all live by faith.

Trust is the norm; it is the only option we really have
to figure out the Truth about our existence. Since absolutely
nothing is 100% verifiable by anybody—from scientist to
guru—by necessity we all trust what we use on this Truth
Journey.

We all trust our eyes, brains, tools, equipment,
theories, methods, predecessors and professors, scientists and
doctors, parents, teachers, and preachers. Sometimes these
prove to be unfaithful, and we lose trust and break faith and
even break hearts.

However, the bits of information we deem
trustworthy, we tend to call "knowledge," socially and
academically. When we find something perpetually
trustworthy, we use words like "fact," "knowledge," "proof,"
or "logical truth."

Many people have long desired to have an end to faith. They hope that a staunch devotion to logic and reason could replace the need for what they call faith, which cannot rely on so-called "proofs." On this matter, G. K. Chesterton says in *Orthodoxy*[1], "It is idle to talk always of the alternative of reason and faith. Reason is itself a matter of faith. It is an act of faith to assert that our thoughts have any relation to reality at all."

To help my students step into this painfully freeing and accurate way to see life and to leave behind the naïveté of shortsighted (often close-minded) blind confidence in "proofs" and of what they think they know with 100% certitude, I ask them to imagine living on an island where everything in life is overtly based on faith. Every day, in every moment, all the people on the island live in an acute, awake awareness that they have a perpetually faith-filled, moment-by-moment existence.

I ask the students to imagine our class as travelers on a ship that wrecks on an island in the South Pacific whose inhabitants behave in this manner. It is intriguing to watch the variety of facial expressions and comments as the students wrap their minds around this imaginary. I fuel the image by saying things like, "They wake up and have to believe that they are getting out of their beds, and then believe that the eggs they are eating are real. They must have faith that their parents are really their parents, and that the coffee is not poisoned, and that their tools will work. They must believe that the sun is actually warming them and that night will come in a few hours…" Some student start to smirk because it clicked. Some are confused and frustrated. Some blurt out, "That would be insane! How could anybody live?" Usually someone will timidly raise their hand and cautiously ask, "Isn't that how we all live every day?" And then someone else says, "No way. I don't have to believe that I ate my eggs this morning; I just ate them." The room erupts with debate and questions…. To refocus the class I hold up my miniature blue and green globe and title the earth as, "Faith Island."

We discuss this until it finally clicks for everybody in the room. Often I will offer an A+ for the class if they can give me something they can prove and perfectly verify with one hundred percent certitude. Not surprisingly, it is fairly short work for everybody in the room to comprehend that all of life for all people all the time is interpreted through the lens of trust and faith. Movies like *The Truman Show*, *Matrix*, and *Inception* often enter the dialogue. Ironically, from me to you to every scientist, mathematician, clergy, guru, imam and skeptic, we all currently live on Faith Island, because faith (trust) is the only option for us every day on this whirling, blue and green ball.

However, despite all the cynicism and brokenness in our world, much is worthy of our trust. A healthy Trust List can give an honest sense of security and confidence to make the most of our grand existence and daily adventures both individually and collectively.

I often end a conversation or my class with asking people to write down what is on their personal trust lists. We talk about what is trustworthy, what should be on the list that is not on it and what is on the list that should be removed. We consider what we do and do not trust and why. I ask if he or she is on anybody else's trust list, and why? We discuss what makes something and someone trustworthy, and we discuss the pain and complexities of broken trust. I encourage them that their "homework" not just for tomorrow, but for the rest of their lives is to develop a strong, healthy, dynamic, and life giving personal trust list.

This might be a great time to put this book down and start a conversation with someone about trust lists. The next scene is about navigating the inevitable trap door that comes with facing the reality of Faith Island and trust. Pick the book back up when you have a solid grasp on the concept of trust and a better idea of what and who you trust.

Reflection

1. What makes someone or something trustworthy?

2. What is on your personal trust list? What do you find trustworthy?

3. What should be on your trust list that is not?

4. Is there anything on your trust list that should be removed?

5. As you contemplate your trust list, why do you trust these things? On what basis are they worthy of your trust?

6. Do you think *you* are on anyone's trust list? Why or why not?

<u>MY CURRENT TRUST LIST</u>

- I trust

- I trust

- I trust

- I trust

- I trust

- I trust

- I trust

- I trust

- I trust

- I trust

- I trust

- I trust

- I trust

- I trust

ACT I, SCENE 4

SUICIDE OF THOUGHT

In 1908, the bold, brilliant, and seemingly prophetic G. K. Chesterton wrote in chapter three of *Orthodoxy*[1], "There is a thought that stops all thought, and that is the only thought that ought to be stopped." The chapter is poignantly titled "Suicide of Thought." It is the end game for the thought-full inhabitants of Faith Island.

For those slipping into the vortex of the suicide of thought, the internal monologue Chesterton is speaking of goes something like this: "Since everything is based on trust and I have no means to verify anything, I cannot be 100% certain of anything. Therefore, I should not even try to figure out this reality thing. And anybody who does try is idiotic–because he or she will never be able to be certain, nor can he or she convince me of the certitude, of anything asserted by either of us. Beyond lack of certitude lies the abyss of everything being unverifiable..."

This is a classic agnostic thought process, and it is the thought process of anybody who would like to wallow in the melancholy, half-hearted depression of latent postmodernism. In the mid to late nineteen-hundreds, the influential thinkers and writers of postmodernism were skeptical about life and existence, particularly the overconfidence and self-absorbed humanism of industrial modernity in early part of the twentieth century. These thinkers freely questioned the validity of everything, including human thought itself. This inevitably led to questioning even the validity of human existence. This forced a philosophical debate on the substance and nature of thought itself. I will admit that it is easy to forget that the postmoderns simply recapitulate the deconstructability of the nature and fabric of reality. They remind us that we all have scissors and seam rippers. In other words, we have the ability to dissect and disassemble our interpretations of reality down to the minute pieces of thoughts and truths that we cling to as real and trustworthy.

Postmodern philosophers assert that our understanding of reality has been pieced together like a village made of Legos. And like a village of Legos, we can take apart the whole thing brick by brick and throw the pieces into a bucket, and we have the ability to reconstruct a whole new village with the same pieces. Interestingly, we easily forget that on some level we actually do live in an existential reality. We have chosen to construct our personal view of the world from the individual thoughts we have chosen to put on our personal trust list, from what we deem trustworthy. This what the entire concept of the Trust List is built upon. Existentialism and deconstructive postmodern thinking explain how we all create our own version of reality (little "r") from our personal perspectives of the world as we build our individual Trust Lists piece by piece.

I find it helpful, with this this in mind, to pause and sincerely honor the deconstructionists and even thank them for clarifying this foundational truth. It is appropriate to give them a high five or fist bump, and then, quite frankly, we need to get on with reconstruction and, more importantly, with living. Hearkening back to G.K Chesterton's chapter[1] on "The Suicide of Thought," Chesterton urges, "We have no more questions left to ask. We have looked for questions in the darkest corners and on the wildest peaks. We have found all the questions that can be found. It is time we gave up looking for questions and began looking for answers."

The positive, encouraging truth gleaned from postmodern and existential thinking is that when a powerful voice calls you to renew your mind or change the way you think, we learn that not only is it possible, we also get a glimpse into *why* it is a viable option for people to truly change what they believe and and to change the way that they perceive reality. However, that being said, the suicide of thought can makes the process of building a trust list vain, arbitrary, and capricious. Postmodern thinking began to blend with an extreme existentialist, philosophy that encouraged humans to *only* focus on one's personal, unique, individual, and thus, irrefutable, interpretation of reality. This has unfortunately convinced enough people to believe that there is no Reality (with a big "R"), but there is only fabricated, individual, unverifiable, subjective versions and perspectives on reality (little "r"). Whether intentionally or unintentionally, they spread a lie, saying that since nothing is 100% trustworthy, it is therefore not worth trusting anything at all. When people are persuaded to believe that there is no Reality – in other words, no objective Truth – they unwittingly embrace the lie that if nothing is perfectly trustworthy, then it is futile to trust anything at all. Fortunately and unfortunately, the reality is that *nothing is 100% verifiable*! And, people are often simply distracted from the important difference between "verifiable" and "trustworthy." Thus, the suicide of thought is a formidable black hole which still permeates our culture.

I know many loved ones who have slid willingly and unwilling into this abyss. The crux of this scene is if you or I believe we have found something absolutely trustworthy, in order to maintain any thoughtful dignity and integrity, we have to admit that our direct access to this so-called "absolutely trustworthy" bit of information is through that which is not 100% trustworthy (our eyes, our brain, our senses). Therefore, we are left with the formidable task of figuring out what is worth putting our trust in and then making the most of our delicate situation..

More unfortunate than this is the hard, dark truth that suicide of thought often leads to suicide of will, and sometimes eventually, body. Fortunately, the truth that our entire interpretation of Reality is based on trust levels the playing field for all of us in every household and culture, like the Faith Island metaphor. Because nobody has the corner on the market or the ability to substantiate their understanding of the Truth, we all have an opportunity to engage in healthy, open dialogue. This feeds compassionate community if we are humble enough to be honest about our inability to completely, objectively verify our own trust lists when we are in conversation with those who are struggling to find something or someone who is trustworthy or those who are trying to change their trust lists.

The only way out of the vortex of the suicide of thought is to actually make a real choice. For the first half of the chapter, Chesterton takes the reader into the suicide of thought. Fortunately, for the rest of the chapter, he helps the reader see how to get out of it. This is a complex matter, philosophically speaking, as you will soon see. But here we go. If we make real choices, then we do actually trust something. The natural result of making a choice for something means something is trusted and other choices and things are excluded. If someone chooses to be a vegetarian, he or she will naturally excluding meat from meals. If I choose to wear my running shoes, I exclude my sandals. If my friend as a theist chooses to trust in Allah and the Koran to explain his existence, then he naturally excludes the primary tenets of atheistic materialism. This is the essence and lifeblood of Trust. If you or I walk out our door, breathe, eat, talk, interact with humans, live a life (even a meager one), we have a trust list because we will be making choices. And when we are making choices, we are exerting trust in that which we are choosing. When we choose we are excluding. As such, we find ourselves somewhere on the grid of these four philosophies with their trust lists and somewhere in their various stories. This is why it can be helpful to see life as a journey of discovery. And, yes, on this journey we may find something untrustworthy and need to make different choices based on our experiences. This chapter is about how and why it is possible to even change our choices.

Keep thinking; keep breathing; keep trusting; keep living; and keep finding what is trustworthy. If we keep the fire lit under the kettle of our thinking, our awareness will boil our thoughts down to meet the Reality in which you and I find ourselves. It is an artfully unique situation with distinctly limited information at our disposal.

We can despair in the midst of this truth or make the most of it. Interestingly, one of my students pointed out that we can also try to distract ourselves from building an effective, functional personal trust list. Whatever your response is, at the very least let us not lie to ourselves through constructing a false sense of certitude in our facts or our, knowledge or our proofs. All of life is based on trust, and we are all on this island of faith together, trusting. Let us, therefore, be aware and intentional and create knowledge and facts and proofs out of that which is trustworthy. Let us remember that we are always trusting these tiny bits of information. Here is where the suicide of thought mutates into generative hope.

"Hope deferred makes the heart sick."

Proverbs 13:12 (ESV)

When hope dies, it makes hearts sick. This is not about not getting what we want; it is about ceasing to hope at all. So here is a bit of hope in a potential arid and dry scene at the beginning of this unfolding drama.

The suicide of thought does not actually exist.

I am glad you kept reading. It is an ironic paradoxical truth. If the suicide of thought kills our ability to think through not trusting anything including our own thoughts, the only way to get there is to trust the thought that our thoughts are not trustworthy.

Thus you are trusting something, that thought. Therefore, it is not the suicide of thought anymore. If you can trust the thought that your thoughts are not trustworthy, then you can trust other thoughts. The key here is that it is a matter of choice. We choose which thoughts to trust based on their effect on our mind, body, and soul. Which thoughts will you choose to trust on your journey?

This is the bedrock core of all existence. We trust thoughts. If you can make a real choice, then this is the time to start choosing which thoughts you are going to trust. This is the adventure of life; this is the marrow and the impetus and the traction of life.

This scene ends with a double irony. If we as humans cannot make real choices, then we cannot go into the suicide of thought, and ironically and terrifyingly we cannot get out of it. This is also why we have to spend some time on this. Without choice, there is no autonomy and no real self-direction. There is actually no real self; there is only an illusory perception of "self" in which there actually is no "self." There is only what one might call awareness.

Choice and trust are the essence of all of meaningful existence. Without these key ingredients, there may be life, but as we will see, what that life is has potent consequences.

ACT I, SCENE 5

WHAT IS REALLY REAL?

Foundations of Reality

As I mentioned earlier, my approach to worldview, and thus, philosophy, is simple and practical. It builds off of and extends the iconic works on the nature and outcomes of our beliefs about Prime Reality generated by Socrates, Plato, and Aristotle. In essence these brilliant minds helped us clearly see that the spiritual (the immaterial) and the material are the two basic ingredients for the fabric of reality. Most philosophers agree that Plato's and Aristotle's works on the nature of Prime Reality are a foundation for all human interaction concerning Reality.

Over thousands of years, humans have developed Trust Lists based on their perspectives of the two options for the substance of Prime Reality: the spiritual world and the material world. As I have mentioned, a logical grid built from these two entities results in the possibility of four foundational

Trust Lists: idealism, materialism, monism, and theism.

This is the tension of the big story we all find ourselves *in medius res* on this planet at this moment. Generally speaking, there are four different story line options that help us make meaning out of our lives. The law of non-contradictions (which states that a thing cannot be true and not true at the same time) and the reality of personal experience creates distinctions in these stories that seem insurmountable. As explained in scene three, we all live by faith. In scene four we saw that no one has the corner on the market when it comes to verifying the truth of his or her story and trust list with 100 percent certitude. Every story and trust list seems to be true, at least to someone, yet we know intuitively and logically that all of the trust lists cannot be true at the same time. My approach is not simply another shallow, slippery attempt to advocate relativism or universalism. Nothing could be further from the point. Even though there are four basic attempts to understand what is Really Real, and from these four basic trust lists (or worldviews), there are hundreds of religions and "isms" and ways, there is ultimately only one True Prime Reality—one real storyline that is the unfolding true story of humanity.

Every great epic adventure story is driven along by tension, and there is plenty here to go around. Thus we have the main plot of our story.

The Tension of the Four Perspectives

We could call these four perspectives the four main characters in this story. The setting is planet Earth, and the plot is the quest for Truth. Each character is vying for the ability to claim victory by being credible and being the most trustworthy—the world view that is the most accurate! Pure idealists trust that only the spiritual truly exists as ultimate, eternal, prime reality. Authentic materialists trust that reality consists exclusively of the measurable material world of the periodic table of elements, electricity, and waves. Complete monists (or pantheists) posit that both realms are real and exist as extensions of each other—although dual in nature, they are essentially one entity with no actual distinctions or real separation. Sincere theists believe both domains exist, but the spiritual realm and the material realm co-exist independently, interdependently, and intra-dependently, with deep connectivity yet real distinctions.

These four perspectives contain and generate all of the isms, religions, ways, beliefs, cults, heresies, ideologies, worldviews, and seekers of Truth. Therefore, every individual will, by necessity, find himself or herself somewhere on the Trust Lists Grid when answering life's essential queries.

In some respects, the Trust Lists are simply another way of organizing and seeing. They provide a fresh, empowering map for navigating life's biggest questions and a concise, effective tool for approaching and understanding the daunting array of worldviews and religions.

We all seek satisfying answers and fulfilling resolution to the natural tensions of daily living. In our search for peace and authenticity, we each trust one of, or perhaps a blended form of a few of the four answers to the big questions posed by philosophy. In this text I chose seven of the main questions humans have to face in a lifespan, no matter how long or short.

Failure to find one's self drawing from these four lists is usually indicative of a lack of awareness of the object of a person's trust or a lack of awareness of the natural consequences of what those answers eventually bring.

Being unaware usually results in feelings of being overwhelmed, underwhelmed, unfulfilled, unfruitful, or angry, bitter, and resentful.

However, an appropriate alignment and awareness of real consequences of our choices—especially concerning the nature of Reality—simultaneously creates unity, peace, and freedom while reducing internal conflict and confusion. An honest assessment of the object of trust and the outcomes of this trust leads to clarity and a deeper sense of ownership and vitality. Thus, this accessible approach to worldviews can be empowering, engaging, freeing, and inspiring.

Reflection

1. What ideas or images stood out to you in this act?

2. What was refreshing? Why?

3. What was frustrating? Why?

4. What questions do you have?

ACT II

TOOLS & TENSION:

PLOT & SUBPLOT

ACT II, SCENE 1

PHILOSOPHY

Philosophy as a Tool

This Trust Lists Grid and the information connected to the grid do not contain any new knowledge. It is simply an opportunity and an invitation into an efficient, effective way of organizing and connecting the information. With this grid, alignment is offered, clarity is gained, and healthy dialogue emerges. Because this tool is rooted in Honor, Respect, and Freedom, all people can gain new hope, joy, peace, introspection, and momentum no matter where they are on their own personal journey to find Truth.

This grid, combined with the essential truths of Faith Island discussed earlier, levels the playing field and invites all into meaningful discourse concerning the consequences of our own choices in relation to what we trust.

Every human being seeks resolution to the tension in the big story of life and one's own tensions in day-to-day living. It is essential to recognize the vital role of trust and the powerful tool of practical philosophy, honest self-examination, and healthy, honoring conversation.

Often the consequences for trusting various options are astronomically different. Those differences are worthy of a closer look and some rich dialogue. The Trust Lists and the Trust Lists Grid are organic. Like all philosophy, the tools are simply a means to an end, not the end itself.

I love this short poem by G.K. Chesterton[1]:

Here dies another day

During which I have had eyes, ears, hands

And the great world around me;

And with tomorrow begins another.

Why am I allowed two?

We are privileged to live our day-to-day lives. This is the unfolding plot of not only this text, but the unfolding story we are in. These pages contain one more approach to making sense of the world and of our daily decisions. Philosophy builds a framework for these decisions. We use philosophy to build a "house" to live in each day, whether we realize it or not. Understanding the four trust lists and some of the big questions is an empowering, manageable, and practical approach towards creating personal ownership and awareness of your own trust list.

This process can be compared to building a house. Philosophy is a tool that helps us build a place to live in everyday reality. Your house that you live in would be what some people would call your religious beliefs, like the Catholic approach to Christianity, or your "ism," like atheism or pantheism. The isms and religions give us the day-to-day framework and context for interacting with people and making daily decisions, particularly concerning morality and relationships. The first act gave us what holds the house together and what the foundation is made of: trust. Trust is the screws, the glue, the nails, the brackets, and the concrete. Act two is about pouring the foundation your house will rest on, axioms and such. It is about the lumber and framework, the plumbing and electrical work that is hidden behind the walls and paint. Act three is where you will see the various options for the type and style of home you want to create, the big questions and their answers connected with their natural consequences. Act three will almost feel like a home decor showroom displaying all of the decorating and detail options.

Sometime during the first week of my class, I hold up my grandfather's antique, leather-handled hammer. My grandfather loved to build. Hammers were meant to build and create. If we are not using philosophy to build and construct our trust lists and worldviews it will look and feel and be ostentatious. It would be like buying a new hammer and a holster belt and then simply carrying it around. Try to picture that. It is painfully awkward. Hammers are powerful, focused tools that are made to drive in nails. Almost anybody can learn to use one. My seven-year-old twins love pounding nails and building birdhouses or fairy gardens. Elijah, Anna's twin brother, loves to *use* his hammer. Another truth of the hammer is that in the process of building, a hammer can be useful for demolition and deconstruction, as mentioned in act one scene four. If I need to renew my mind and change my perspective, I can use philosophy as a hammer to carefully pull apart the nails and boards of what I have trusted to create space for an addition or a new kitchen, or a new way to see the world. I could also take a sledge hammer and swing away to create space for a whole philosophical extreme makeover.

Because philosophy is a tool, it has neutral moral value. Consider a common item like a cell phone or a car. In and of themselves they are morally neutral—neither good nor evil. Therefore, as a tool, their value, usefulness, and moral implications rest in the intent and motivation of the user. Just like a hammer could be used to build a beautiful home or helpful in much-needed renovation or repairs, it could also be used to smash windows or even skulls. It is one thing to hit your own thumb (or another person's) on accident when aiming for a metal spike. It is another to intentionally smash someone else's thumb with the hope of breaking it. Thus we all have to be hyper-vigilant to use the powerful tool of philosophy in a safe, honoring, loving, generative, and creative way. Pretense with philosophy makes you and I look like a fool. The misuse of philosophy makes you and I cruel. There has been and is too much abuse and cruelty cause by a misuse of philosophy, let alone theology, doctrine, and religion. The *abuse and misuse* of philosophy is toxic and destructive; it spreads fear and confusion, and it poisons everything.

There are many voices that echo down to us about the profound power of a tool such as philosophy, a tool that has the power to help you find what is trustworthy and let go of destructive thoughts and weak, fruitless premises. Margaret Mead says: "Never doubt that a small group of thoughtful, committed citizens can change the world. Indeed it is the only thing that ever has." One of my favorite quotes in the spirit of this scene is from Mahatma Gandhi. He pointedly says: "Be the change you want to see in the world." And I will end this scene with a declaration from Anne Frank: "How wonderful it is that nobody need to wait a single moment before starting to improve the world." Improving your own perspective of the world is a great way to start improving the world.

ACT II, SCENE 2

AXIOMS

Axioms on the Nature of Reality

The stage is set with piles of bricks and stones. Construction materials are strewn about. A half-finished frame, recognizable as the skeleton of a house looms in the background. There are graceful pillars standing apart. A huge hole has been dug into the earth ready for a strong foundation...

To continue with the metaphor, philosophical axioms are the foundations on which we build our houses. They are the pillars, or rocks, or the cement castings on which we build our daily lives. These statements of truth are often the basement of our thinking and living, hidden underground. But they are essential, because everything is resting on them. If they are faulty, the whole house is suspect or unstable. Thus, an axiom is self-evident and irrefutable. A solid foundation lets us build a solid house. A solid foundation gives stability and confidence. Strong, clear axioms help create confidence and trust. Good axioms are a fountain of trust and trustworthiness.

An axiom or postulate, is a premise or starting point of reasoning. As classically conceived, an axiom is a premise so evident as to be accepted as true without controversy[1].

An axiom is an unprovable rule or first principle accepted as true because it is self-evident or particularly useful[2]. For example, one common axiom is, "Nothing can both be and not be at the same time and in the same respect". It should be contrasted with a theorem, which requires a rigorous proof. The Big Bang theory or the theory of Natural Selection are both theorems.

Consider a few foundational axioms:

AXIOM: The law of non-contradiction states that contradictory statements cannot both be true in the same sense at the same time.

AXIOM: If there is no spiritual realm or objective reality to the material world, then morality by necessity has to be internally subjective (relative) in a closed system of cause and effect.

AXIOM: If morality is internally subjective in a closed system, then, the concepts of right and wrong, good and evil, fair and unfair, are arbitrary and absurd. All of morality is ultimately based on perceived personal preference.

As I describe a few more useful axioms it is important to define a key term. Perfection is a challenging word to explain, but for the purposes here I want the word to mean what almost all of the dictionaries start with and with what most people intuitively think of in regards to the concept. The word perfection used here is the state or quality of which something or someone cannot be improved upon, a condition of having no flaws. It is derived from such words as completeness, fullness, and wholeness.[3]

AXIOM: A perfect Being must have perfect standards; therefore, one must be perfect in order to dwell with this perfect Being or to exist as this perfect Being.

AXIOM: If an eternal state of perfection exists, then, if one is not perfect, one must become perfect in order to exist in a state of perfection or to experience an eternal state of perfection

AXIOM: An imperfect being cannot become perfect perfectly if left to himself or herself, because one would need to be perfect in order to do this perfectly.

AXIOM: If all that exists in the cosmos is matter and electricity expressed through pure cause and effect relationships, then existence for humanity is completely subject to cause and effect and autonomous independent freedom of choice (free will) cannot exist.

AXIOM: If there is no actual distinction between a universal spirit and the human spirit, then there is no individual, autonomous human spirit and consequently there is no individual free will for humans.

AXIOM: Authentic grace is a completely free gift; therefore, the offering of this pure gift cannot be dependent on the receiver's attitude, behavior, motivation, perspective, understanding, ability, character, ethnicity, comprehension, intelligence, actions, etc. to receive this gift.

There are vast numbers of philosophical axioms. I chose to put a few here that I thought were useful to expose. They make for strong healthy conversation and they are trustworthy, tried and true. These axioms, all axioms, are meant to be pondered upon and agreed with; and then they should fade to the background, or even underground like a foundation. Let them settle in, especially for this journey through this book. They should feel rock solid, firm, embedded, and comfortable. A natural response to an axiom would be, "Yes, of course… that's obvious." Or, "I never thought about it like that before, but that makes total sense."

If you do not understand one of them or why they matter, consider the subtitle of this text: "Conversations on the Trust List." Go start a conversation with someone about the ones that do not seem to fit or the ones that don't click. If they do make sense, consider letting them stand strong and solid, like a flying buttress on an ancient cathedral that has beautifully supported massive walls for hundreds of years. Smack it like an I-beam in a warehouse when you walk by it, ponder its strength and glance up at what it is supporting, and then move on to the next scene…

ACT II, SCENE 3

FUNCTIONAL TRUTH

Buckets of Truth

It is essential to understand that there are two functional and accepted types of truths.

Speaker and teacher Mike Penninga[1] created a simple and effective metaphor to clearly explain the essential functional differences of subjective and objective truths. He states that various truths can end up in two different "Truth Buckets."

Subjective and Objective

Each of us must take ownership for understanding the life-effecting consequences of our personal choices regarding the truth bucket into which we place various Truth statements.

Many people who approach philosophy and theology for the first time, or even over a lifetime, confuse this issue. Worse yet, many people have built a lifestyle from various philosophies and theologies, especially concerning morality, with a deep misunderstanding of this foundational approach to reality.

Consequently, people consciously and subconsciously put universally trusted objective truths into their own personal subjective buckets. When building a house to live in, philosophically speaking, it is important to use the right materials at the right time in the right way. With axioms off kilter or not solid, we end up with a Leaning Tower of Pisa or a cracked, crumbling, leaky basement. When we confuse objective and subjective, it is like mixing mortar that is unsuitable for building a wall out of bricks. It will look solid, but it will be weak and unsafe. When we lean on the wall or put any pressure on the wall, it will wobble and most likely come crashing down with devastating effect. When confronted with consequences for life-affecting decisions and lifestyles, there may be painful social consequences. Often the person who has made this mistake is blind or ignorant to this misappropriation of truth and what they are trusting, so they feel awkward at best and utterly foolish or defeated at worst when light is shed on the mistake. The personal emotional and spiritual consequences are often grave; morality decisions and discussions surrounding sexuality, abortion, slavery, and stealing which can be strong examples of this common error.

In light of some of these issues, unfortunate and devastating personal and communal negative consequences can result from a simple lack of awareness or from intentional ignorance and denial about the healthy practice of appropriate differentiation of the buckets into which we place Truths. Furthermore, this responsibility has exponential impact on leaders! Teachers, parents, and mentors must clearly and continually articulate into which bucket they are putting the various lessons they teach.

Subjective truths are purely based on the perspective of the subject (person) making the decision; they are relative concepts based only on personal preference, opinion, and perspective. These truths tell us more about the subject (the person and his or her feelings or opinions) than the object (the issue or item) in question.

For example: A person's preferred ice cream flavor is a subjective truth. This subjective truth has everything to do with personal (subjective) preference or opinion about the object and is not describing the nature of the object, ice cream.

Some truth statements based on subjective truth are:

- Vanilla ice cream is the best flavor.
- Your stained glass window is beautiful and inspiring.
- Ice cream is delicious.
- It is a beautiful day outside.
- Grandma is mean and rude.

Objective truths are purely based on that which is true regardless of the perspective or feelings of the person making the decision or observation; it is a universally trusted standard.

These truths are focused entirely on the object in question rather than the subject (the person and his or her perspective, feelings, or opinions about the item or issue).

For example: Insulin's effect on lowering blood sugar levels to help with diabetes is a trusted objective truth. This objective truth has nothing to do with personal (subjective) preference or opinion and is entirely based upon the nature of the object, insulin.

Some truth statements based on objective truth are:

- Insulin lowers blood sugar levels and can help manage diabetes.
- The stained glass window is broken.

- There are a wide variety of ice cream flavors.
- It is sunny and seventy degrees outside with a gentle breeze.
- Grandma did not give me the gift I wanted.

As we work our way through act two, the design of this act and these scenes is to become familiar with the tools for building our worldview home and personal trust list and lean into the tensions of the plot on our search for Truth. In many respects the tensions should be tightening, because as we move into act three we will see that there are real choices to be made with real differences and profound, life-affecting consequences connected to those choices. In his plays, Shakespeare often waits until the end of act one and often into act two to reveal the full weight of the plot of his stories. I hope that you feel like all of this is becoming clearer as we finish setting the stage (Faith Island), continue to get to know the four main characters (the trust lists), develop the plot (our collective search for Truth and a clear picture of Prime Reality), and start unearthing the sub-plot (your individual development of a firm and functional personal trust list). Let's look at some essential information on morality and the concepts of perfection before we head into act three.

ACT II, SCENE 4

PERSPECTIVES ON PERFECTION AND MORALITY

Communicating a Common Definition

One of the essentials to understanding the significance of our individual trust lists in our daily lives is to understand how the words *perfection* and *morality* are defined.

Each of the four trust lists provide individual perspective on the definitions of perfection and wholeness. These definitions shape not only our perception and understanding of reality, but they also shape how we relate to each other on a daily basis.

When we fail to understand that four different people in a single conversation may be utilizing the same word to describe separate perspectives, we delve into a world of misunderstanding based in false assumption.

Four Perspectives on Perfection

As mentioned earlier when we were considering a few philosophical axioms, *perfection* is a challenging word to explain. For the purposes here I want the word to mean what almost all of the dictionaries start with and with what most people intuitively think of in regards to the concept. The word *perfection* used here is the state or quality of which something or someone cannot be improved upon, a condition of having no flaws. It is derived from such words as completeness, fullness, and wholeness.

Idealism:

> For pure idealists, perfection and wholeness comprise an objective ideal state of being, based on the nature of the "Spiritual Ideal" This is because idealists trust that only the ideal spiritual realm is really real. For them, it is something other than the substance of the material realm which does not last. The stuff of the material world breaks or is broken already; it is not ideal and can always be improved upon. For idealists, perfection is that which is eternally good, beautiful, and true. It is eternal because it is perfect and will last forever in that state. And quite frankly, not that it matters, we would want it to last forever, because it is perfect. It is that which has no flaw;

it is the only standard by which all things are measured. According to Plato and the tenants of Platonism, there can be only one "form" of perfection. For idealists, perfection is objective like the insulin example from act two scene three. It exists as true and perfect whether humans like it, know it, appreciate it, etc.

Imagine the ideal car or chair. It never runs out of gas, never breaks down, and never rusts. It is perfectly smooth and efficient and so on. That car does not exist on earth, yet. But what are all of the idealistic car makers trying to create? That car. The idea of a car will last longer than any physical car will. Actually, if all the cars on the planet vanished, the idea of that car would still remain! We could almost call this trust list "idea-ism."

It really hits home when I ask my students to close their eyes and imagine the perfect human being. They chuckle and laugh; they quietly ponder; and then they open their eyes as we discuss this ideal being. They can all talk about a perfect human being, but nobody has met one. I ask them if any of them thought of themselves when their eyes were closed. In twenty years of teaching, nobody has ever had the image of their current self come to mind (or the courage to admit it publically).

This is a big step in understanding the trust list of an idealist. The imperfect exists in the unsubstantial material realm on this entropy-filled planet. If we want to exist forever, we must strive until we actually become that one, perfect ideal that is spiritual, not physical.

Materialism:

For an authentic materialist, perfection and wholeness are literally in the eye of the beholder, and therefore they are utterly and completely relative and subjective. Because there is no outside, objective standard for perfection, and because everybody has his or her own unique, individual, personal perspective on the world from within the world, materialists have no authoritative, purely objective standard for making verifiable comparisons. People can agree on standards, or they can pretend that there is objectivity, but this is fabricated and malleable. It is like the ice cream flavor debate. When I take my family to the ice cream store it would be ridiculous for Elijah to tell Anna that mint chocolate chip is the perfect flavor and that Anna's preference for chocolate chip cookie dough is subpar, incorrect, and imperfect. We cannot say that a rose is the perfect flower and that a thistle is imperfect. Well, I guess we can, but we would be simply stating our opinion and nothing more.

Monism:

For a complete monist perfection and wholeness are part of existence; therefore, everything is perfect as it exists. This is similar to the materialist perspective on perfection; it simply adds in the weight of spirituality. Monists will concede that there is nothing objective, above, beyond or separate from all of the universal united collective coexistence of everything. Consequently, the concept of perfection is always subjective, because there is nothing that is distinct from the unified existence of the universe. As such, monists do not believe in an all-powerful creator or artist or God in the sense that theists do, so there is no basis for any objective comparison or standard. Often a monist will refer to existence with authoritative vocabulary like "god" or "the unifying life force." A monist believes everything in existence to be a part and parcel of god who in nature fits the definition of perfection as that which cannot be improved upon. Therefore, everything is perfect as it is, if only we had the eyes and willingness to see it as such. To continue with the metaphor, all ice cream flavors are perfect just as they are, if you could only see from the right perspective. All of that which exists is perfect simply because it exists.

Theism:

> Perfection and wholeness exist as defined by an objective, perfect, living Being. This Being is the standard and creates the standard. This Being is perfect, cannot be improved upon, eternal, and complete. This Being is objective, distinct and independent, from creation and from created beings. This is similar to idealism, but instead of a state of existence, or an abstract concept, "form," or idea, this Being is alive, interacts with creation and created beings, and has authority over these other beings. Thus, there is the potential for unlimited, independent definitions of perfection and wholeness as defined by this objective, perfect Authority.

In theism, this Being is usually referred to as God. C. S. Lewis notes in *Mere Christianity* that, unlike monism, in theism God is separate from creation like an artist is separate from a painting. In monism, everything is god, there is not separation or objectivity; the painting is god and god is the painting. Monists would say that the painting is alive and perfect as it is and we are all a part of that unfolding living painting, kind of like a film without a director. Theists say that God is a being and is alive, and God decided to create a work of art that is alive yet distinct from his Being; we are our own beings.

Therefore, as an artist God has the objectivity and authority to decide or declare what is perfect. Thus, humanity is subject to God's definition of and standards for perfection. This is a great place to see an axiom come into play: Because God is perfect, God will have perfect standards; therefore, one would have to be perfect to dwell with this perfect Being.

Another interesting point on perfection for theists surfaces when created human beings reject or differ on their interpretation of or relationship with God the perfect standard of perfection.

Reflections on Perfection

This scene in our story is focused on various perspectives of perfection. In the course of our unfolding story, we need to remember that someone who has a different trust list then you may use the same word you use with vastly different consequences.

Why don't we give this a peek. Imagine four characters having a cup of coffee and discussing perfection. An authentic materialist and a complete monist would get along pretty well as they discuss the differences and similarities on what is perfect. There is no heaven or hell or objective standard, just undiluted freedom to describe perfection based off of whatever standard is preferential.

The pure idealist and the sincere theist would have to debate the standards and the sources they trust to define what is perfect, be that an enlightened teacher of sorts, a sacred text, a moment of awareness, or a trusted system of religion. The theist and the idealist will differ when discussing access to this standard. A theist could, if desired, discuss access to this standard through a personal relationship with this Living Being called God. An idealist will most likely describe this standard as a state of being, and if the tem god is used it is in the literal, strict sense of the definition of perfection above. While a theist spends time with God in a relationship, this state of perfect existence that an idealist calls god is not a Being or a persona that an idealist could hang out with. An idealist strives to become one with this ideal one existence. An idealist would need to become god and become perfect in order to exist as god. For the theist, because this perfect God Being has perfect standards, the theist would need to become perfect according to God's standards in order to dwell with this God. A theist never becomes God. Again, conversations between a theist and an idealist would naturally turn into a discussion on the methodology for attaining and sustaining this state of perfection.

The philosophy does not necessarily show us what the religions believe and practice; it shows us *why* religions do what they do and offer what they offer. It also shows us why a conversation between a theist and a monist on what perfection means will have vastly different outcomes than conversations between a theist and a theist or an idealist and a materialist. When we layer the objective and subjective concepts with ideas like perfection and standards for morality, the contrasts and the chasms start to get much wider and deeper.

Four Perspectives on Morality

Like perfection, morality is a challenging word to explain because of the types, layers, implications, and functions of morality. In this book, we will focus on the daily decisions of practical morality concerning right and wrong and good and evil often referred to as *ethical* morality. What we are most concerned with is where the authority and standards come from for these decisions. Do we simply get to decide what to do with our time and money and bodies? Or does someone else decide? Or does an objective, absolute standard exist for everybody to follow?

Idealism:

For a pure idealist, morality is objective based on the nature of the spiritual Ideal as eternally good, beautiful, and true. Moral behavior and decisions are defined as right and good based on the perfect ideal of what is good, beautiful, and true. However, morality feel subjective for idealists living on Faith Island based on each person's imperfect and incomplete personal interpretation of and limited access to the spiritually ideal, objective standards of what is perfectly good, perfectly beautiful, and perfectly true. It is intrinsically difficult for that which is imperfect and, broken, unformed, and ugly to know and understand, let alone do and be, perfectly good, beautiful and true.

Materialism:

For an authentic materialist, morality is subjective at the core, similar to the explanation of perfection. It is internal and relative based completely on perspective and preference, like choosing an ice cream flavor. Because there is nothing objective outside of and distinct from the cause and effect nature of the material realm, morality appears to be based on self (on individual humans) with no actual, real, objective authority or standards. However, for the vast crowds of authentic materialists, morality feels objective when powerful people or organizations enforce individual or group preferences, or when a community gives authority to a majority or a select group of people. This feeling of objectivity can be subtly misleading for many materialists. Such moral standards are not actually objective; rather, they are the result of subjective majority preference.

Monism:

For a complete monist, morality is wholly subjective and is basically the same as that of a materialist. The difference is that the weight of one's preference often carries greater authority, because a monist can claim to be part of the universal being often called "god." In short, good and evil, right and wrong behavior and standards are based on the understanding of self as being part of the collective universe which exists as god. The self is part of the universal, absolute authority of humanity's collective coexistence. However, morality for a monist, like that of a materialist feels objective when moral "preference" is universally established, usually through human loyalty or majority rule. Moral standards can be objectified by tradition and rituals or by allegiance to a preferred aspect of behavior or a preferred standard. This often ends up manifesting itself in the form of allegiance to a "side" drawn from the dualistic and polarized nature of reality on planet Earth, such as light and dark, birth and death, creation and decay, etc...

Theism:

For a sincere theist, ethical morality for humans is objective based on the nature of the Creator God as the definer of and standard for Morality. However, because God is an autonomous Being separate from creation and from created beings, morality is actually subjective for God who has the intrinsic power and authority to define morality. It is important to note that for most theists, God is perfect, and thus has perfect morality and perfect standards for morality. This is important, because perfection as we have defined it in this context is that which cannot be improved upon and that which has no flaw. It is complete and whole. Therefore, although God is a living Being, God will never change moral standards, because moral standards are perfect as they are and cannot be improved upon. They will not change because they will never need to change because they have no flaws.

Interestingly for theists, morality often feels subjective in a similar way that perfection can feel subjective since it is based on one's personal interpretation of and limited access to God, God's nature, God's Word, and God's revelation. This is where different religions and denominations within these religions can have a wide variety of moral standards, but all of them say they are based on God's perfect standards. And, once again, we are abruptly reminded of the intricacy of living together on the large, round, spinning Faith Island.

As act two comes to a close, I hope you can feel the plot thicken a little. While there may be elegant overlap and interplay between these different trust lists, and some of the answers to life's questions are almost identical on the different lists, there are also differences that are polar opposites and even diametrically opposed to each other. I hope you can see why I started the journey starts in act one with the basic tenants of Faith Island. We all are trying to figure out this stuff as best we can using what we deem as trustworthy. Learning about the critical differences between these four worldview perspectives should help us humbly approach conversations with a listening ear and an open heart. It is of vital importance to firmly plant a stake in what you trust to be true.

Paradoxically, it is of vital importance to remember that what you believe to be true is *believed*; it is *trusted*, not "proved" or "100% objectively verified." With this in mind, it is time to explore the different trust lists. It could feel like a house tour...

Reflection

1. What ideas or images stood out to you in this act?

2. What was refreshing? Why?

3. What was frustrating? Why?

4. What questions do you have?

ACT III

FOUR VIEWS OF REALITY:

THE TRUST LISTS

ACT III, SCENE 1

TRUST LISTS

The Power of a Question

Language is powerful. Conversations can and do change the world, but without common understanding the words we use in conversation can become unproductive or even divisive as people talk around each other instead of dialoging with each other.

A foundation for understanding and conversation begins with an agreement about the nature of the two essential elements in the composition of reality, material and immaterial. With this, we can then build four possible lists of conclusions from each of the four possible perspectives. As each of us unearths our own understanding of what we deem to be worthy of trust, we can begin dialoguing with others.

Human beings throughout history have wrestled with finding answers to questions about the true nature of reality. These questions have to do with the natural details of life as it unfolds or unravels each day. The information in the

82. Inklings.

following pages is my best attempt to accurately and honorably represent how each of the four perspectives and stories of reality respond to seven of the big questions regarding reality. While there are many more questions that we must wrestle with individually and in community, these seven reflect questions that every human has asked, is asking, or will one day need to ask in order to help us not only understand ourselves but to further pry open the door to creating the type of understanding that will lead to further dialogue.

I also hope that this text can loosen the tongues of those who want to become more comfortable with openly conversing about those questions some of us tend to shy away from—the big, hard, life questions. Fear, a fallacious belief in unsatisfying half-answers, dislike of the answers available, and the fact that all answers to these big questions are entirely based on trust, undoubtedly unsettles one's nerves.

I try to set up my classroom as a place where we can ask and lean into any of life's hardest and most complex questions. I learned the value of such a classroom space from one of the most inspiring literary criticism professors I have ever had, Dr. Charles Bressler. In college, he introduced me to the basic structure of these four worldviews and the big questions of philosophy. He trained his students to analyze and interpret literature written from each of these views and also to read critically through the lenses of these views. It was life transforming, and I owe him credit for planting the seeds of this trust list tool. Furthermore, in an effort to give credit and honor where it is due, you should be aware that the big questions of philosophy you find in this book look very similar James Sires' in his influential book *The Universe Next Door*[1]. Although Sire did not originate the big questions of life, he and many other philosophers made them colloquial, as they should be, and I tip my hat to them!

These are the questions every human asks (or should be asking) while they tread the terra firma, soar through the stratosphere, or spiral into space. More than once, my young sapling twins have plumbed the mysteries of the universe in these "big questions," be it the death of our beloved pet, or a reason to share toys and food, or the impetus of the unceasing, "Why, Papa?" We are naturally inquisitive as a species. Sire did not invent the questions of philosophy (none of us did), yet I honor and applaud him and his work in generating a broader dialog. These questions, all questions, are the natural response to what life throws at thoughtful, introspective, aware, autonomous beings.

I have reworked what I believe to be some of the big ones here for the focused purposes of this "Trust List" tool. They are meant to represent the big questions, not define them. I am sure we could come up with twenty big questions, or boil them into three, or even one. That is not the point: rather, the point is that we all have questions and that there are thoughtful answers for us to choose from. The rub is that the answers are all based on Trust, they are often very different, and they are usually polarized in conjunction with their varied, natural, inevitable, daily consequences. Ultimately we are all using what we trust to make sense of reality as we perceive it. The consequences we encounter based on the trust list we each adopt directly relates to what we have put our trust in. Therefore, what we trust about reality has magnificent importance in our daily lives.

It is helpful to remember the four different "characters" (trust lists) and the houses they build for daily living through how they each approach the questions we are looking at in this text. The four trust lists are:

- Pure idealism, which looks at only the spiritual as really real.

- Authentic materialism, which trusts in only the measurable material realm.

- Complete monism, which accepts both the spiritual and the physical realms as fully real with complete unity and no authentic distinctions.

- Sincere theism, which believes in the reality of both the

spiritual and the material reals as connected but with real distinctions.

These four views of Prime Reality have to address every question, every day, by everyone! The answers to the questions chosen in this book have overarching implications throughout the entire storyline of someone's life. They also serve as excellent examples for getting familiar with how this tool functions. Hopefully you will become skilled at using this tool so you can apply it to any question anyone might have anywhere at any time. These seven questions provide a venue for practicing the use of this approach to understating world views. The questions are:

1. What is the nature of Reality? What is really Real?

I have found this is a great place to start all conversations concerning world view. This is where the four options find their roots and distinctions. Most of the other questions will find the core of their answers directly in relation to this question.

2. Who or what is God?

Everybody has to interact with this question. Depending on what you trust to be true, God may be a concept, a vocabulary word, a theory, a person, a spiritual being, oneself, the unnamable and unknowable, the creator... I have found that most popular atheists understand that even if they do not believe in God, they still have to directly interact with other people who do, and they still have to deal with the popular vocabulary word and concept that has infused our global conversation.

3. Who is man? What is mankind? What is a human being?

We all have asked or are asking, "Who am I?" and, "What am I?" These are foundational questions and they have profound implications, particularly in relation to the other questions listed here. Are we individuals? Are we distinct? Are we free beings, or are we a connected part of something or someone else...or both? Are we puppets or self-directed or not directed at all?

4. What is the basis of and standard for morality? How do I decide between right and wrong, and where is the basis for moral authority?

This questions begs whether or not morality is even objectively real. If so, where did it come from and why do I have to obey a moral code? This is why authority is a critical part of this question. Does a moral code have any real authority over me, and if so, why? If an ethical moral code does exist, can I change it? Why would I submit to an ethical moral code that I did not make?

5. What happens to a human at death?

Death permeates our world. What is death? This question surrounds us everywhere. Is it something to be feared or embraced? Is death an end or the beginning of a new adventure or the continuation of this adventure? Does death offer hope or does death end hope? Is death simply a concept, or is it a vocabulary word? Can I define death however I choose, or is it defined for me?

6. What is the meaning and purpose of human history? What is the essence of human interaction and relationships?

I kept this question as part of this tool because we have memories, individually and collectively, and they affect us profoundly. This question helps us understand and define meaning. When seeking answers to the question of history, we are drawn into the popular struggle for understanding the mystery of origin. This also gives more perspective on the concept of story with a beginning and possibly an end...

7. Why are we here? Where are we going? What is the purpose of human existence? To be or not to be? What is the purpose of living for tomorrow?

I think this is the question that most of us are either enjoying, pursuing, denying, dreading, or despairing over. It is the one that is often the most personal and most powerful. I have found from personal experience that the answer to this question sets the tone and atmosphere for day to day living. It effects everything. Like a soundtrack for a musical or a movie, it creates the backdrop of the stage. Literally and figuratively, it creates the mood of the house we choose to live in.

In the rest of this scene are found the lean version of the answers of the four different trusts lists. It lends itself to brief compare and contrast. Imagine you have just entered a large house for a big party. The following few pages can be compared to being introduced to various people. Some of these people you know well and are happy to see. You feel comfortable connecting with their familiar faces. Some of these people you have heard about (even in the past few scenes) and are now actually meeting. Some of these people (and their corresponding worldviews and trusts lists) you have already pre-judged and you have a predisposition either for or against.

As you read and converse with others when you put the book down or participate in discussions, you will find it helpful to keep the tone as though it were a celebration of sorts, a party or a feast. Do not be the one who crashes the party with hate, rudeness, or dishonor. We are guests in someone else's house. You do not have to agree with everyone at the party or all of the views expressed on the following pages. (If you did so, you would actually be confused and not only look foolish, but also be considered a fool.) Here, in this book, everybody is in the same room for a bit so we can all get to know each other better in a safe, healthy way through open dialogue and fruitful, meaningful conversation. In short, these brief introductions can allow students and readers to get a feel for the tone and the landscape of each worldview. In the following four scenes we will take a deeper look at each of the four trust lists.

7 Essential Questions

1. What is the nature of Reality? What is really Real?

IDEALISM (Platonism)

A pure idealist trusts that only the spiritual is really real. Reality is a state of eternal spiritual perfection.

MATERIALISM (Atheism)

An authentic materialist trusts that only the material (the natural) is really real; there is no spiritual realm.

MONISM (Pantheism)

A complete monist trusts that the spiritual and the material are both really real, existing as one entity without any actual distinction. Reality presents itself as dual in nature, yet all of existence is ultimately one, universal, interconnected unity.

THEISM (Monotheism)

A sincere theist trusts that the spiritual and the material are both real, yet they are independent (self-reliant and separated from one another), interdependent (collaboratively and reciprocally reliant on each other), and paradoxically intradependent with each other (unified and reliant upon each other as a collective whole, like a body with integrated dependent parts).

2. Who or what is God?

IDEALISM (Platonism)

A pure idealist trusts that the impersonal, eternal, perfect spiritual ideal is what people often call "god." It is absolute, complete truth, beauty, and, goodness.

MATERIALISM (Atheism)

An authentic materialist trusts that there is no objective, powerful being outside of the material. God is a figment of man's creativity and imagination, a creative idea or concept.

MONISM (Pantheism)

A complete monist trusts that everything is "god." Because there is no distinction between anything, there is no distinction between god and humans and the fabric of the universe. Everything and everybody in the universe is an integral, interconnected part of the unity of life called "god."

THEISM (Monotheism)

A sincere theist trusts that there is a distinct God who is the all-powerful creator, sustainer, and giver of all of life. God is personal and has personality.

3. Who is man? What is mankind? What is a human being? (Who am I? What am I?)

IDEALISM (Platonism)

A pure idealist trusts that humans exist as one of the infinite, incomplete, imperfect replicas or shadows of the real, eternal, ideal state of spiritual perfection.

MATERIALISM (Atheism)

An authentic materialist trusts that human beings are a fascinating, unique, and highly complex system of matter and electricity that is beautifully aware of self and others.

MONISM (Pantheism)

A complete monist trusts that a human is a unique unrepeatable part and parcel of "god." We are part of the body of the universe and the entirety of reality referred to as "god."

THEISM (Monotheism)

A sincere theist trusts that humans are a distinct, wonderful creation made in the image of God but not possessing the exact nature of God nor existing as an extension or part of God.

4. What is the basis of and standard for morality. How do I decide between right and wrong, and where is the basis for moral authority?

IDEALISM (Platonism)

A pure idealist trusts that all morality is objective and based on the nature of the impersonal, perfect, spiritual ideal, which is absolute truth, perfect beauty, and complete goodness.

MATERIALISM (Atheism)

An authentic materialist trusts that all morality is ultimately subjective and based exclusively or collectively on self, majority, and power.

MONISM (Pantheism)

A complete monist trusts that morality is completely subjective based solely on one's individual preference and as a part of the interconnected, universal reality called "god." Thus, morality is completely relative, yet it appears dual in nature due to the complexity, polarities, and variety found in the universe.

THEISM (Monotheism)

A sincere theist trusts that all ethical morality is objective based on the personal, all-powerful nature of God who is Perfect and Good. God (and, by extension, God's word and God's nature) is the standard for and author of morality. Many sincere theists follow ritual moral codes, distinct from ethical moral codes pertaining to personal and collective religious beliefs.

5. What happens to a human at death?

IDEALISM (Platonism)

A pure idealist trusts that when we die, perfection is attained. We become one together in a unified state of spiritual perfection, and (or) we cease to exist as a shadow of perfection and as an imperfect "self."

MATERIALISM (Atheism)

An authentic materialist trusts that humans cease to be aware of one's existence at the point of death.

MONISM (Pantheism)

A complete monist trusts that when a human dies we literally morph into another part of existence and another component of the universal reality, which is god.

THEISM (Monotheism)

A sincere theist trusts that when humans die, we obtain and sustain individual perfection and exist eternally in continual relationship with the perfect, personal God; or, we remain in an imperfect, incomplete state and necessarily exist separated from a perfect God.

6. What is the meaning and purpose of human history? What is the essence of human interaction and relationships?

IDEALISM (Platonism)

A pure idealist trusts that history and human memory are records of humans striving to escape nonexistence and attain an ideal state of spiritual perfection.

MATERIALISM (Atheism)

An authentic materialist trusts that history is a story of a linear sequence of events and phenomena linked by cause and effect in a closed system (such as natural selection). Human interaction is literally chemistry and pure cause and effect.

MONISM (Pantheism)

A complete monists trusts that history and human memory consist of the repository of collective memories of our collective coexistence as god.

THEISM (Monotheism)

A sincere theist trusts that history is a "linear, meaningful sequence of events leading to the fulfillment of God's purposes for man" in an open system[1]. History is the true, epic, adventure story of God's interaction with mankind; it is the real story of life that we are participating in.

7. Why are we here? Where are we going? What is the purpose of human existence? To be or not to be? What is the purpose of living for tomorrow?

IDEALISM (Platonism)

A pure idealist trusts that we exist only to achieve and sustain an ideal state of spiritual perfection.

MATERIALISM (Atheism)

An authentic materialist trusts that humans create their own individual and collective meaning for life.

MONISM (Pantheism)

A complete monist trusts that every human has the exciting opportunity to continue experiencing being various components of universal reality—of god—forever.

THEISM (Monotheism)

A sincere theist trusts that at least one reason that humans exist is to enjoy and experience a meaningful relationship with the Creator and Sustainer of Life.

ACT III, SCENE 2

A CLOSER LOOK AT PURE IDEALISM

We are striving to exist as spiritual perfection, the Spiritual Ideal (as God or as part of God).

Pure idealists trust that only the spiritual is the eternal fabric of prime Reality. True idealists have a foundational understanding that the non-material, "perfect ideal has an eternal, beautiful, true, and good weight and realness to it that supersedes any physical attempt to replicate and materialize this true idea.

This understanding leads them to a greater awareness that this weight or realness of the ideal is manifested in a spiritual reality and is merely, often poorly, represented (re-presented) in the physical.

For all of the physical world, but particularly for humans, this situation is accurate. Humans are essentially

imperfect shadows or incomplete imitations of the Spiritual
Ideal. Humans are literally trying to become one with ultimate
reality, which is an enlightened state of spiritual perfection.
Currently, humans are imperfect and exist on earth only as
representations of imperfect images of perfection. In essence,
we exist as potential. A pure idealist would say we have the
opportunity to achieve eternal existence in a state of perfection
in the Ideal Spiritual realm if we can achieve this state of
perfection.

To illustrate this highly abstract concept in my classes,
I ask the students to make a shadow on a table with one of
their hands. Is the shadow real? What is the substance of the
shadow? What is the shadow made of? The shadow is totally
dependent on the hand, and the hand is not dependent on the
shadow at all. The shadow exists, if it exists, because of the
hand, not vice versa. In the course of this discussion, I ask the
students to try to pick up the shadow with their other hand. I
announce, "Welcome to idealism!" The hand is the spiritual
realm, and the shadow represents the material realm. If the
shadow wants to exist forever, it must become the hand.
Otherwise it will cease to exist when the light changes.

Similarly, look at an image of yourself. Try to imagine
the processes that that picture would need to undergo to
actually become you and not just an imperfect, incomplete

image of you. To an idealist's way of thinking, humans are personally responsible for making themselves into the Ideal, for becoming perfectly good, beautiful, and true. In this state, individuals will exist fully and eternally as spiritual perfection. In so doing, they will eternally escape the fate of nonexistence as an incomplete, shadowy replica.

Below is a list of some religions, "isms," and ways that construct trust lists from this worldview. With this information in mind, it you can learn more about why people of certain religions and "isms" make the choices they do concerning day-to-day living and lifestyles. you may find it instructive to further research these and to have some conversations with people who have adopted these lifestyles.

- Buddhism
- Much of Hinduism
- Taoism

Answering the Big Questions of Life:

Another Look at the Philosophical Trust List of a Pure Idealist

1. What is the nature of Reality? What is really Real?

A pure idealist only trusts that the spiritual is really real and that Reality is a state of eternal spiritual perfection. The material realm is an imperfect, incomplete, shadowy replica of the Ideal. In other words, the material realm is a broken, twisted, and warped shadow of the Ideal, which is absolutely good, perfectly beautiful, and purely true.

2. Who or what is God?

A pure idealist trusts that the impersonal, eternal, perfect, one Ideal is what people call "god." It is absolute, complete truth, beauty, and, goodness. God is a state of mind and a state of existence. God is the Ideal One that is perfect absolutely and forever. God is the Ideal state of being that is the pursuit of humanity.

3. Who is man? What is mankind? What is a human being? (Who am I? What am I?)

A pure idealist trusts that humans are not perfect; we are one of the infinite, incomplete shadows of the real state of spiritual perfection; humans exist simply as potential to become one with the Ideal and to finally exist as the perfected Ideal in a state of eternal, spiritual perfection and completeness.

4. What is the basis of and standard for morality? How do I decide between right and wrong, and where is the basis for moral authority?

> A pure idealist trusts that all morality is objective based on the nature of the impersonal, perfect Spiritual Ideal, which is absolute truth, perfect beauty, and complete goodness. All thought and behavior is aimed at achieving and sustaining this state of existence.

5. What happens to a human at death?

> A pure idealist trusts that when we die, perfection is attained and unity or oneness with the Ideal is achieved. We realize our potential, let go of the imperfect representation of self, and become one with the state of spiritual perfection. We cease to exist as an imperfect self and shadowy broken representation of perfection. We simply cease to exist materially on Earth. Individually, we cease to exist at all.

6. What is the meaning and purpose of human history? What is the essence of human interaction and relationships?

> A pure idealist trusts that history and memory are a record of humans striving to escape nonexistence and attain an ideal state of spiritual perfection. Human interaction is summed up and actualized in striving to escape nonexistence, either alone or together.

7. Why are we here? Where are we going? What is the purpose of human existence? (To be or not to be? What is the purpose of living for tomorrow?)

A pure idealist trusts that we exist only to achieve and sustain an ideal state of spiritual perfection, to escape painful non-existence, and to exist eternally through becoming one with the Ideal One. This is accomplished by existing eternally as absolutely, perfectly good, beautiful, and true in, and as, the Spiritual Ideal.

ACT III, SCENE 3

A Closer Look at Authentic Materialism

We are our own individual gods; there is no objective God to become, to serve, submit to, or to dwell with. We simply are.

Authentic materialists trust that the composition of Prime Reality is only that which can be observed and measured materially. No real spirituality or spiritual realm exists. Humans are beautiful, complex systems of matter and electricity who are subjected to an intricate arrangement of pure cause and effect and awesomely aware of their immediate, unfolding presence in time and space.

The impression of perfection or of the Spiritual Ideal is a completely subjective, relative concept. Consistent materialists believe that humans can do and be whatever they prefer, so long as they avoid negative natural consequences. Simultaneously and paradoxically, they acknowledge that this freedom is arbitrary, and that it is ultimately a façade. Life is actually an unfolding, passive adventure of random, electronic, reactionary impulses.

Consistent and authentic materialists unabashedly and wholeheartedly embrace the idea that life is ultimately absurd and beautifully or grotesquely ridiculous. Therefore, genuine materialists assert that humans can attempt to create their own sense of adventure, purpose, and meaning. Humans live out their awareness in the most personally pleasurable ways available while seeking to achieve positive natural consequences and avoiding negative natural consequences.

Below is a list of some religions, "isms," and ways that construct trust lists from this worldview. With this information in mind it you can learn more about why people of certain religions and "isms" make the choices they make concerning day-to-day living and lifestyles. You may find it instructive to further research these and have some conversations with people who have adopted these lifestyles.

- Atheism
- Humanism
- Existentialism
- Phenomenology
- Nihilism

Answering the Big Questions of Life:

Another Look at the Philosophical
Trust List of an Authentic Materialist

1. What is the nature of Reality? What is really Real?

An authentic materialist only trusts that the material (the natural) is really real; there is no spiritual realm. Matter and electricity have existed eternally in various forms and states without beginning or end. That which is observable and measurable is really real.

The spiritual realm is a chemical, electrical figment of the human imagination; the spiritual can represent all we have yet to discover how to measure and understand.

2. Who or what is God?

An authentic materialist trusts that the individual human is his or her own god. There is no creator God in the universe as the authentic materialist perceives it. The general definition and attributes of god either disappear as unreal ideas or those characteristics transfer to humanity.

There is no objective, powerful being outside of the material. God is a lovely or an ugly lie, a figment of man's creativity and imagination, or a generative creative idea or concept.

3. Who is man? What is mankind? What is a human being? (Who am I? What am I?)

An authentic materialist trusts that human beings are a fascinating, unique, and highly complex system of matter and electricity that is beautifully aware of self and others.

Mankind is currently the pinnacle of existence in an infinitely intricate system of cause and effect. Mankind is the amazing realization of the ongoing potential of matter and electricity.

4. What is the basis of and standard for morality. How do I decide between right and wrong, and where is the basis for moral authority?

An authentic materialist trusts that all morality is ultimately subjective and based on self, majority, and/or power. Morality is essentially absurd at the core. There is no a truly objective standard for good and evil for humans, nor can there ever be. Therefore, all morality is essentially relative, based on value and agreed submission to (or rejection of) a constructed system of human authority, community, and power.

5. What happens to a human at death?

An authentic materialist trusts that humans cease to be aware of one's existence at the point of death. There is no eternal existence of one's spiritual soul beyond the grave, because there is no eternal spiritual soul dwelling in the human body.

6. What is the meaning and purpose of human history? What is the essence of human interaction and relationships?

> An authentic materialist trusts that humans, individually or collectively, create our own meaning for existence.
>
> History and memory are ultimately absurd with no objective, overarching meaning or purpose. History is a story of a linear sequence of events and phenomena linked by cause and effect in a closed system (such as natural selection).
>
> Human interaction is chemistry and pure cause and effect.

7. Why are we here? Where are we going? What is the purpose of human existence? (To be or not to be? What is the purpose of living for tomorrow?)

> An authentic materialist trusts that we create our own meaning for life. At the core life is essentially, objectively absurd, because no objective meaning or purpose does nor can exist.
>
> Humans live for whatever brings pleasure or the hope of pleasure.
>
> We hope for or create beneficial change of circumstances with the goal of increasing positive and decreasing negative natural consequences.

ACT III, SCENE 4

A CLOSER LOOK AT COMPLETE MONISM

We are already part of god (the Universe). Embrace and enjoy this truth and stop striving to become what you already are.

Complete monists trust that both the measurable material and mysterious spiritual realms co-exist as one (very large) entity. Monists, often called pantheists, assert that all of Reality is one reality presenting itself as dual in nature. This duality is represented in unlimited perspectives and polarities as experienced throughout the vast complexity and tensions of life.

For a complete monists, all of life is connected. Humans are part of all existence, and all of that which exists is already the Ideal for life. Thus, humans are already perfect as various parts of the one entity that monists often refer to as god.

God literally is everything, and humans are part of the everything that exists. For all of Life:

Emotions = Spirit = God = Truth = Life = Material = Perspective = Emotions.

Like a human body that has many apparent distinctions and parts yet maintains a complex unity and harmony, so is the universal reality and unity of monism.

Humans each embody unique perspectives of god. Humans have unlimited potential and power as god or as a connected part of god.

Humans embrace their unique preferences and seek a balance of all perspectives and polarities so as to wake up, realize, and utilize their true identity and unity.

Humans (along with all creatures and all parts of reality) grow in awareness of all perspectives as they embody the simplicity and complexities of life as part of the one, gigantic self.

Humans learn how to see all of life and all of life's tensions and polarities—the dualities of life—as a valid and valuable part of humanity's collective unity and coexistence with all that exists.

Below is a list of some religions, "isms," and ways that construct trust lists from this worldview. With this information in mind, you can learn more about why people of certain religions and "isms" make the choices they make concerning day-to-day living and lifestyles. You may find it instructive to do some further research on these and have some conversations with people who have adopted these lifestyles.

- Pantheism
- New Age
- Much of Hinduism
- Tribal religions that worship nature
- Theosophy

Answering the Big Questions of Life:

Another Look at the Philosophical Trust List of a Complete Monist

1. What is the nature of Reality? What is really Real?

A complete monist trusts that the spiritual and the material are both real, existing as one entity.

The spiritual realm and material realm both exist, but they are one and the same. There is no separation or distinction.

Reality presents itself as dual in nature through polarity and perspectives. However, all of existence is ultimately one universal, interconnected unity unfolding in various forms.

2. Who or what is God?

A complete monist trusts that everything is god. Everything and everybody in the universe is an integral, interconnected part of the unity of life called god.

Existence and reality are what people often call god. The cosmos is filled with duality and polarity as manifested in all of life; thus god has a dual nature in essence and in being.

3. Who is man? What is mankind? What is a human being? (Who am I? What am I?)

A complete monist trusts that a human is a unique, unrepeatable part and parcel of god. We are part of the body of the universe and the entirety of reality appropriately referred to as god.

Man is not truly distinct and separate from god, but man exists as part of reality and the cosmos which, in essence, is part of the entire being of god.

4. What is the basis of and standard for morality. How do I decide between right and wrong, and where is the basis for moral authority?

A complete monist trusts that morality is completely subjective based 'souly' on one's individual preference as a part of the interconnected, universal reality called god. Like god, as god manifested in the universe, morality is dual in nature. That is to say, god and morality are positive and negative energy, creative and destructive forces, darkness and light, heat and cold, et cetera, ad infinitum.

5. What happens to a human at death?

A complete monist trusts that when a human dies, that person morphs into another part of existence and another component of reality, which is god. The shared, united soul shifts into another part of the cosmos with another unique perspective on living as god.

6. What is the meaning and purpose of human history? What is the essence of human interaction and relationships?

> A complete monist trusts that history and memory consist of the repository of collective memories of our collective coexistence as god. Humans are connected to history as part of the unfolding story of the cosmos which is god.

7. Why are we here? Where are we going? What is the purpose of human existence? (To be or not to be? What is the purpose of living for tomorrow?)

> A complete monist trusts that every human has the exciting opportunity to continue experiencing being various components of universal reality—of god— forever. We are here to wake up to who we are as a unique part of god and reach our full potential as our part of the divine existence and unity of god.

ACT III, SCENE 5

A CLOSER LOOK AT SINCERE THEISM

We are unique individual creations hoping to become perfect (or complete) so as to dwell with God, our Perfect Creator.

Sincere theists trust that both the spiritual and the material are components of Prime Reality. While they are interdependent and dependent with one another, they are also mysteriously intradependent, or, in other words, dependent within each other. Humans are unique, individual creations in the image of a free, independent, personal, and all-powerful Creator often referred to as God.

Although humans are created in the image of the one, perfect God as individual, distinct creations of God, humans are independent beings from God, and they do not possess the exact nature of God. Humans are created to dwell freely with God and enjoy a relationship with God and God's creation.

On earth, humans exist as imperfect, incomplete beings, essentially separated from God's perfect identity and standards. Therefore, in order for humans to escape eternal separation from their perfect Creator and to dwell perpetually with their perfect Creator, individual perfection and fullness must be achieved and sustained.

Below is a list of some religions, "isms," and ways that construct trust lists from this worldview. With this information in mind, you can learn more about why people of certain religions and "isms" make the choices they make concerning day-to-day living and lifestyles. You might find it instructive to further research these and have some conversations with people who have adopted these lifestyles.

- Judaism
- Islam
- Christianity
- Tribal religions that worship a Creator

Answering the Big Questions of Life:

Another Look at the Philosophical Trust List of a Sincere Theist

1. What is the Nature of Reality? What is really Real?

A sincere theist trusts that the spiritual and the material are both real, yet they are independent and interdependent with each other. The spiritual realm and material realm are both independently real, yet they coexist and interact independently, interdependently, and intradependently within each other in various, forms, degrees, and in diverse ways.

2. Who or what is God?

A sincere theist trusts that there is a God who is the all-powerful Creator, the sustainer, and the giver of all of life. God is perfect and essentially good in nature and being. God is personal and has personality. God has full authority. God is the standard for and author of morality.

3. Who is Man? What is Mankind? What is a human being? (Who am I? What am I?)

A sincere theist trusts that humans are a distinct, wonderful creation made in the image of God, but humans do not possess the exact nature of God nor do they exist as an extension or part of God.

4. What is the basis of and standard for morality? How do I decide between right and wrong, and where is the basis for moral authority?

A sincere theist trusts that all ethical morality is objective based on the personal, all-powerful nature of God, who is perfect and good. God is the standard for and author of morality, as are God's word and God's nature. Though this does not necessarily have to, this may include ritual traditions or cultural norms that many would call ritual morality.

5. What happens to a human at death?

A sincere theist trusts that when humans die, one of two things will occur based on our choices in this life. Either we will obtain individual perfection and exist eternally in continual relationship with the perfect, personal God, or we will remain in an imperfect, incomplete state and necessarily exist separated from God. When we die, we actualize our True self and exist with God, or we are eternally separated from perfection and wholeness.

6. What is the meaning and purpose of human history? What is the essence of human interaction and relationships?

A sincere theist trusts that history is a "linear, meaningful sequence of events leading to the fulfillment of God's purposes for man" in an open system[1] History is the true, epic, adventure story of God's interaction with mankind. It is the real story that we are in right now. Humans are independent, autonomous, and gregarious, possessing will and identity as self in communion with others.

7. Why are we here? Where are we going? What is the purpose of human existence? (To be or not to be? What is the purpose of living for tomorrow?)

A sincere theist trusts that at least one reason humans exist is to enjoy and experience a meaningful, personal relationship with the Creator and sustainer of life.

We exist in order to expand, enjoy, and protect God's kingdom. We exist so we can bring joy and honor to God and self through genuine worship of God, through loving healthy relationships with God and others, and through authentic serving of God and others.

ACT III, SCENE 6

INTERVIEW A FRIEND

In the spirit of healthy dialogue, take this book and these questions and go have a friendly conversation. Start the process of getting to know what other people trust. Become familiar with the language and behaviors others around you use to express their trust lists. I recommend you do this with more than one person, for practice, and more importantly, for gaining insight into different perspectives. I believe that the most important aspect for this part of the story and your journey as we wrap up act three is to have a listening ear and to exhibit honor and kindness. Keep in mind that we intentionally set the tone for this scene as a party or celebration, not a courtroom! Take notes and ask sincere questions. No arguing or defending, just questions, listening, and learning. You are a guest in someone else's philosophical house.

Ask.

Listen.

Honor.

Connect.

Learn.

The Philosophical Trust List of: _____

Big Questions of Life

1. What is the nature of Reality? What is really Real? Ask the person who you are interviewing to talk about both the material and the spiritual realms.

2. Who or what is God?

3. Who is Man? What is Mankind? What is a human being? (Who am I? What am I?)

4. What is the basis of and standard for morality? How do you decide between right and wrong, and where is the basis for moral authority in your daily decisions?

5. What happens to a human at death? What do you trust will happen when you die?

6. What is the meaning and purpose of human history? What is the essence of human relationships?

7. Why are we here? Where are we going? (To be or not to be? What is the purpose of living for tomorrow?) Why do you believe you exist? And what do you exist for?

ACT III, SCENE 6

MY TRUST LIST

Take some time to ponder the answers you have for yourself in this act. It might help to have someone interview you. It also might help to carve out some solitude time or to go for a walk. Remember, the most important part of this list is integrity and honesty.

ASK – LISTEN – HONOR – CONNECT – LEARN

Big Questions and Big Answers of Life for Me

1. What is the nature of Reality? What is really Real? Consider both the material and the spiritual realms.

2. Who or what is God?

3. Who is Man? What is Mankind? What is a human being?
(Who am I? What am I?)

4. What is the basis of and standard for morality? How do I decide between right and wrong, and where is the basis for moral authority?

5. What happens to a human at death? What do I trust will happen when I die?

6. What is the meaning and purpose of human history? What is the essence of human relationships?

7. Why are we here? Why am I here? Where are we going? Where am I going with my life? (To be or not to be? What is the purpose of living for tomorrow?) What do I exist for?

Reflection

1. What ideas or images stood out to you in this act?

2. What was refreshing? Why?

3. What was frustrating? Why?

4. What questions do you have?

ACT IV

THE FULLNESS OF REALITY AND THE FINISHED STORY:

"THE MAN"

"There is a huge and heroic sanity of which

moderns can only collect the fragments.

There is a giant of whom we see only the

lopped arms and legs walking about.

They have torn the soul of Christ into silly strips,

labeled egoism and altruism, and they are equally

puzzled by His insane magnificence and

His insane meekness.

They have parted His garments among them,

and for His vesture they have cast lots; though

the coat was without seam woven from

the top throughout."

G.K Chesterton
Orthodoxy[1]

ACT IV, SCENE 1

THE FULLNESS OF CHRIST

The *Treachery of Images* is a painting by the Belgian surrealist painter, René Magritte. The picture shows a pipe. Below it, Magritte painted the words, "Ceci n'est pas une pipe." This is French for, "This is not a pipe."

I propose that for humans there is a similar treachery of Reality (and theology and doctrine for that matter). The Truth is found in a person, not in a list of trustworthy answers to big questions. The Truth is not found in a book about a person or even they very words of that Being. The picture of a pipe is not a pipe; it is a picture.

So often, we stop at the pictures of reality or the stories about reality. C.S. Lewis famously put it like this in his indelible sermon, *The Weight of Glory*:

> "In speaking of this desire for our own far off country, which we find in ourselves even now, I feel a certain shyness. I am almost committing an indecency. I am trying to rip open the inconsolable secret in each one of

you—the secret which hurts so much that you take your revenge on it by calling it names like Nostalgia and Romanticism and Adolescence; the secret also which pierces with such sweetness that when, in very intimate conversation, the mention of it becomes imminent, we grow awkward and affect to laugh at ourselves; the secret we cannot hide and cannot tell, though we desire to do both. We cannot tell it because it is a desire for something that has never actually appeared in our experience. We cannot hide it because our experience is constantly suggesting it, and we betray ourselves like lovers at the mention of a name. Our commonest expedient is to call it beauty and behave as if that had settled the matter. Wordsworth's expedient was to identify it with certain moments in his own past. But all this is a cheat. If Wordsworth had gone back to those moments in the past, he would not have found the thing itself, but only the reminder of it; what he remembered would turn out to be itself a remembering. The books or the music in which we thought the beauty was located will betray us if we trust to them; it was not in them, it only came through them, and what came through them was longing. These things—the beauty, the memory of our own past—are good images of what we really desire; but if they are mistaken for the thing itself they turn into dumb idols, breaking the hearts of their worshipers. For they are not the thing itself; they are only the scent of a flower we have not found, the echo of a tune we have not heard, news from a country we have never yet visited."

I have taught philosophy to high school students in a private school setting for many years. As I share the four major worldviews in which we humans trust, I come back again and again to this concept penned by Lewis and to the opening quote by Chesterton. As I teach my students that each worldview is but a portion of the Truth—though we trust in our worldview and hold to it as if it were the whole—I am convinced more and more deeply that the fullness of Truth and Reality are found only in the undivided person of Christ. I believe that you and I shall know the Truth and the Truth shall make us free, and I believe the Truth is not a fact or a premise or an axiom or a philosophy; it is a Person. The truth is a living, loving being.

Within the specific context of not being deceived by weak philosophy, bad doctrine, and shallow hearsay, the apostle Paul pens the following to the new church in Colossae: "For in Him all the fullness of Deity dwells in bodily form, and in Him you have been made complete" (Colossians 2:9-10 NASB).

I have the Bible on my trust list. As I read through the New Testament, I find that one of the main messages, if not the main message, is a compelling invitation to trust that the man, Jesus, is the Truth. He is the one who will help us understand what is Really Real, because *He* is Really Real.

Many of us need to make the leap from trusting information about the truth to trusting the Truth Himself.

We need to go from trusting a list of trustworthy statements about Reality to trusting the fullness of Reality.

This book is not an attempt to be the truth... it is mean to point to the Truth.

This too is not a pipe!

ACT IV, SCENE 2

IMAGES AND METAPHORS: TRUTH WITH A TWIST

Truth, like gold, is obtained not by its growth, but by washing away from it all that is not gold!

Leo Tolstoy

Chesterton poetically references John's account of the crucifixion when he says at the end of chapter three, "The Suicide of Thought," in *Orthodoxy*[1], "There is a huge and heroic sanity of which moderns can only collect the fragments. There is a giant of whom we see only the lopped arms and legs walking about. **They have torn the soul of Christ into silly strips,** labeled egoism and altruism, and they are equally puzzled by His insane magnificence and His insane meekness. They have parted His garments among them, and for His vesture they have cast lots; though the coat was without seam woven from the top throughout."

The Fullness of Christ and Reality

While philosophy has both value and potential, it also can be heady, wordy, and hard to manage. This has been an attempted to translate it and break it down a bit so you can piece it back together and have a greater understanding of the fullness of Reality, and ultimately you may understand Grace and Truth while utilizing the power of paradox to live with intention as you continue on your journey. Keep in mind that real love and real honor allows you to do all of this in authentic, healthy, life-giving community.

Just like René Magritte said that a picture of a pipe is not a pipe, this list of trustworthy truths is not the Truth. It is a list of Truths about the Truth Himself. It is a list of trustworthy sayings that can point you to the living Truth who is worthy of your trust. Even as the Apostle John wrote out his words about the Word Himself whom he knew personally, ate meals with, and loved; he knew that what he wrote was a bunch of words that can point you to The Word who became flesh, who became the Son and dwelt a while among us and who is seated at the right hand of the Father.

To continue with the house metaphor, the book thus far has hopefully helped you construct a philosophical dwelling place, a worldview home of sorts built of that which is trustworthy. This act is meant to be a starting point for becoming or living as a Christ-Centered Theist. As a Christ follower, I intentionally point my students and readers to Jesus. This is where I hope my students and readers will invite the Living Truth into the house that you have built or are building. The truth is not the house that you used the hammer of philosophy to build, nor is it the trustworthy axioms and solid trust lists you are utilizing. The Truth is a Person you get to invite to live in your house with you. This is the same Person who built the universe and who ate fish on the beach with a few of his friends two thousand years ago after he redefined death for the entire human race. He is the author of life and of the story we are all in. You and I can communicate with Him about the story we are creating.

Remember, this approach to philosophy is an artifact, a tool. These four trust lists and stories point us to a person. My book, any book, is not the truth. It is a tool intentionally trying to point to the person of Christ, to the Truth as the Living, Incarnate, Fullness of Reality. Philosophy is a tool, a means to an end—and that end is Christ. This book renders a disservice if it simply gives you more information but doesn't point you to the person of Christ.

As you read, you may be trusting in a piece of the truth, not the Truth itself. Ultimately, we need to get beyond the clothing and the tunic to the Man Himself. This book is just clothing. These lists are just His garments. The one without seam is a great metaphor for the person of Christ. For some of us, that relationship might start with crawling through the dust to His feet like Mary did in the movie, *The Passion of the Christ*.

For others it may be like the awkward hug Mary gives Jesus in the garden after the resurrection. I love that hug, because it is a person she is hugging. It is not information; it is not a story; it is not a trust list or a philosophy or a doctrine or theology about Jesus. It is Mary hugging a living, breathing, human being: Jesus.

John is a poet. In great poetry, the details matter. I do not know why John said that the cloak was divided into four parts (John 19:23-24). I am not sure any of us can know this side of eternity without direct special revelation. Nevertheless, I want to capitalize on that detail. Although I do not know why he shared that Jesus' clothing was divided into four parts, but in light of the concept that Prime Reality can be dissected into four parts, it is convenient that he did.

Of course, people who are clinging tightly to a section of the garment of the fabric of reality, people like you and me, will often claim with fervor, "I do not have a *piece* of reality. What I have is the Truth, and I have it all figured out."

Paradoxically, those who arrogantly claim with the utmost belief that they are right are often the ones who have the hardest time letting go of the "silly strip" they are clutching and learning to embrace the living, breathing, fullness of Reality. I know this painful truth from personal experience. Unfortunately, many people are content clinging to the clothing, unlike Mary Magdalene in the garden who we find clutching the risen Savior Himself. John describes the moment in chapter twenty of his gospel account in verses 11-18 (NIV):

> Now Mary stood outside the tomb crying. As she wept, she bent over to look into the tomb and saw two angels in white, seated where Jesus' body had been, one at the head and the other at the foot.
>
> They asked her, "Woman, why are you crying?"
>
> "They have taken my Lord away," she said, "and I don't know where they have put him." At this, she turned around and saw Jesus standing there, but she did not realize that it was Jesus.
>
> He asked her, "Woman, why are you crying? Who is it you are looking for?"

> Thinking he was the gardener, she said, "Sir, if you have carried him away, tell me where you have put him, and I will get him."
>
> Jesus said to her, "Mary."
>
> She turned toward him and cried out in Aramaic, "Rabboni!" (which means "Teacher").
>
> Jesus said, "Do not hold on to me, for I have not yet ascended to the Father. Go instead to my brothers and tell them, 'I am ascending to my Father and your Father, to my God and your God.'"
>
> Mary Magdalene went to the disciples with the news: "I have seen the Lord!" And she told them that he had said these things to her."

Importantly, salvation is by grace, and grace is a glance, a trust, a belief, a hope, a surrender. It is not dependent upon the depth of a relationship or the strength of the hug. And yes, as seen in another story about Jesus's clothing, even the "hem of His robe" is powerful. But in that story, Jesus pauses and turns to the woman who grabbed at his garment and tenderly calls her "daughter;" he engages in a relationship with her (Matthew 9:20-22):

> Just then a woman who had been subject to bleeding for twelve years came up behind him and touched the edge of his cloak. She said to herself, "If I only touch his cloak, I will be healed."

Jesus turned and saw her. "Take heart, daughter," he said, "your faith has healed you." And the woman was healed at that moment.

When we finally arrive at clasping the Real Being himself in our own way and in our own time, this Savior, Friend, and King, the living Truth Himself, will probably respond to each of us in the same way that he did to Mary in the Garden in that moment of powerful embrace. We might find Him saying something like "Stop clinging to me; stop clutching me; stop hugging me so tightly. Enough with the bear hug. I love hugs, I really do, but let me see your beloved face. Let us walk together and talk. I have more to give you then simply a hug." Similarly, we often grip a saying or a tweet or a quote that is true. In so doing, we do not proceed forward to the logical next step. We often stop at salvation by faith and grace, and we miss His loving face and embrace.

You may be wondering, as I found myself pondering, "What will we do when we move past the verbiage and finiteness of language and words into relational connection with the living God of the universe?" What happens when we move past simple salvation into graceful relationship?" I believe that this is ultimately what we are longing for, and this is what we were made for. In the story of Jesus, and thus Christianity, this is essentially what we have been invited into. If this is what you want, to hug the living, loving, embodiment of reality Himself, to have a conversation with God and to receive His unquenchable fulfilling love, then this book, like a compass, is meant to point you towards Him. It is not to simply give you more words about Him. If you want to interact with fabric, metaphors, or paintings, you may find the pages of this book interesting, but you will have missed the entire point. You will have the picture of a pipe and not a real pipe. You will have words but not The Word.

As mentioned earlier in this book, I do not want to create straw men and simply knock them over. The intention is not to use apologetics to ruin other people's worlds or worldviews. This approach is about addition, not necessarily subtraction. I know that demolition is an important part of rebuilding with the Truth. I also personally know the powerful destruction that partial truths can bring, the key is that I am not focused on that in this text. There are other texts on this topic and ultimately The Holy Spirit of Christ is the expert at that work.

Ultimately this is paradoxically about a Person, not the paintings or the garments, nor the words. But if you have followed the trail of my thought in this scene thus far, let me keep leading you to the practical focus of piecing together the parts of this journey from act three into act four. If you have a "strip" of Christ's garment as Chesterton calls it, it is still a piece of Christ's garment! Consider a painting such as *The Last*

Supper, by Leonardo da Vinci. If such a work of art were parceled into four sections, having a piece of the Truth is like holding a part of the masterpiece.

If you have any section or even a piece of it, it is still a piece of the original. It is still a piece of the Truth. However, having a section of the truth while thinking it is the entire picture is unsettling when the Truth is revealed. The consequences of basing all of our daily decision in life on this piece of reality, on a strip of the truth, on partial understandings and limited information, has profound consequences.

I am propose, in light of Christ, that the piece you may have is still only a section of the Original. Even if you have the section with Jesus pictured in it (as many Theists do), it is still only one part of the whole painting, not the full painting itself. Even more so, I had to come to the excruciating realization that on my journey I was, figuratively speaking, putting a painting of Jesus on my wall instead of getting to know the living Being Himself.

My hope is that whatever strip or piece of section of the Truth you cling to will ultimately point you to the Truth Himself. And when you bring your rent rags to Him, may you find that the truth you cling to is made complete only in Him.

You will not be disappointed but astounded in the truth you found and the truth He adds to what you are clutching to. You may find that you simply drop what you are holding in order to hold onto or be held by Him.

This book is simply an invitation to the greatest party, to the best relationship, the most full life, to the best way to live. Get to know a person, the Person. Act five will offer a few more practical tools to help guide you on your journey towards Truth.

I end this long scene with a few more words from the seventeenth chapter of John. These words that Jesus prayed before his journey to the cross are potent:.

> "But now I am coming to you, and these things I speak in the world, that they may have my joy fulfilled in themselves. I have given them your word, and the world has hated them because they are not of the world, just as I am not of the world. I do not ask that you take them out of the world, but that you keep them from the evil one. **They are not of the world, just as I am not of the world. Sanctify them in the truth; your word is truth.** As you sent me into the world, so I have sent them into the world. And for their sake I consecrate myself, that they also may be sanctified in truth. I do not ask for these only, but also for those who will believe in me through their word, that they may all be one, just as you, Father, are in me, and I in you, that they also may be in us, so that the world may believe that you have sent me.

The glory that you have given me I have given to them, that they may be one even as we are one, I in them and you in me, that they may become perfectly one, so that the world may know that you sent me and loved them even as you loved me. Father, I desire that they also, whom you have given me, may be with me where I am, to see my glory that you have given me because you loved me before the foundation of the world.

O righteous Father, even though the world does not know you, I know you, and these know that you have sent me. I made known to them your name, and I will continue to make it known, that the love with which you have loved me may be in them, and I in them."

John 17:13-26 (ESV)

Reflection

1. What ideas or images stood out to you in this scene?

2. What was refreshing? Why?

3. What was frustrating? Why?

4. What questions do you have?

ACT V

THE UNFINISHED STORY:

CONVERSATIONS ON THE TRUST LISTS AND LIFE AS AN EPIC JOURNEY AND ADVENTURE

Some inspiring words from Bilbo as the company leaves Rivendell...

I sit beside the fire and think
of all that I have seen,
of meadow-flowers and butterflies
in summers that have been;

Of yellow leaves and gossamer
in autumns that there were,
with morning mist and silver sun
and wind upon my hair.

I sit beside the fire and think
of how the world will be
when winter comes without a spring
that I shall ever see.

For still there are so many things
that I have never seen:
in every wood in every spring
there is a different green.

I sit beside the fire and think
of people long ago,
and people who will see a world
that I shall never know.

But all the while I sit and think
of times there were before,
I listen for returning feet
and voices at the door.

J.R.R. Tolkien
The Fellowship of the Ring[1]

ACT V, SCENE 1

CONSEQUENCES OF BELIEF

This book represents an ongoing, organic dialogue that has been and is being perpetuated since Plato and Aristotle. The debate on Christ as the fullness of Reality has been vibrant and alive since the days of Paul's conversations all throughout the Roman Empire. Take a look at his colloquy with the citizens in Ephesus who believed in "The Unknown God" as seen in chapter seventeen of the Acts of the Apostles.

"Now while Paul was waiting for them at Athens, his spirit was provoked within him as he saw that the city was full of idols. So he reasoned in the synagogue with the Jews and the devout persons, and in the marketplace every day with those who happened to be there. Some of the Epicurean and Stoic philosophers also conversed with him. And some said, "What does this babbler wish to say?" Others said, "He seems to be a preacher of foreign divinities"—because he was preaching Jesus and the resurrection. And they took him and brought him to the Areopagus, saying, "May we know what this new teaching is that you are presenting? For you bring some strange things to our ears. We wish to know therefore what these things mean." Now all the Athenians and the foreigners who lived there would spend their time in nothing except telling or hearing something new.

So Paul, standing in the midst of the Areopagus, said: "Men of Athens, I perceive that in every way you are very religious. For as I passed along and observed the objects of your worship, I found also an altar with this inscription, 'To the unknown god...'"

Acts 17:16-23 ESV)

A similar conversation is continuing here and must continue with honor and dignity. We need to respect each other's free will and right to choose.

The main goal of these final scenes is to create a repository of information to start or continue conversations on the real and often potent consequences of the various trust lists, including a Christ-Centered Trust List. The weight of these pages will be found in the concept of a cost-benefit decision. This not an exhaustive list of the complexities of the costs and the benefits of trusting various answers to the big seven questions used in this book. But it is meant to be thought-provoking and conversation worthy. All of life is a journey, and we are all at different places on our journey. Act two is specifically meant to give practical hands and feet to the abstract concepts laid out in this book. This last act is designed to give examples as to how to process the information in the all of the previous acts. While it is a conclusion to this text; it is really meant to be the start or continuation of your adventure and pursuit of Truth.

Much of the adventure is filled with perpetually learning how to renew our minds and learning how to think differently. It all starts with learning how to Trust something and even Someone new, not just with our heads but also with our hearts, and ultimately with our whole beings. This takes time, dialogue, thoughtful contemplation, surrender, outside help, and the vital process of being on the journey of a lifetime.

ACT V, SCENE 2

TRUTH REVEALED

TENSION RESOLUTION

*"I have been asked to tell you what Christians believe, and I am
going to begin by telling you one thing that Christians do not need to
believe. If you are a Christian you do not have to believe that all the
other religions are simply wrong all through. If you are an atheist
you do have to believe that the main point in all the religions of the
whole world is simply one huge mistake. If you are a Christian, you
are free to think that all these religions, even the [strangest] ones,
contain at least some hint of the truth."*

C.S. Lewis
Mere Christianity

If all of these four trust lists are pieces of the truth or at
least contain pieces of the truth; if they are all parts of the
masterpiece and they are grounded and rooted in Prime
Reality, then it is worth a closer look at the fragments of truth
that are revealed in each worldview.

Here is sampling of this concept to start you on your journey of connecting with Truths from a Christ-centered trust list revealed and embedded in all worldviews. They are listed here in bulleted format to invite discussion and contemplation. Think on and discuss these statements in the context of the trust lists from act three.

Some Christ-Centered Truths Revealed in Idealism:

- Individual perfection and wholeness is the goal.

- Spirituality is really real.

- God is absolute.

- Truth and beauty and goodness are absolute.

- Objective reality exists.

- Much of this world is shadow and dust.

- Human have a dead self, a shadow of our new self found only in Christ.

- Neo-Platonism is a powerful concept for connecting Plato's texts with scriptural truths.

Some Christ-Centered Truths Revealed in Materialism:

- Jesus is fully man!

- Life is absurd without God.

- Morality is defined by the objective Creator.

- We desire real freedom.

- Biologically we have no free will.

- The material realm is Really Real.

- Time, space, and matter exist and are real.

- Jesus Christ has a real, physical body and we will spend eternity with Him in real, physical bodies.

Some Christ-Centered Truths Revealed in Monism:

- The Holy Spirit indwells those who have been redeemed by the blood of Christ and unites believers under the headship of Christ.

- Although we have material and immaterial distinction, we are literally connected through waves, light, and molecules.

- The spiritual realm is real and powerful!

- The material realm is real and lasting.

- There are many polarities and seasons to life.

- We are all one in Christ!

Some Christ-Centered Truths Revealed in Theism:

- God is to be worshiped.

- We are not God; we are created to reflect God.

- God is relational and has being.

- Humans have distinction and separateness.

- There is no self or free will or true morality or love or pleasure or reason without the self, without the soul, and without free will.

- We need to be separate from God yet like God in order to have real intimacy with God.

ACT V, SCENE 3

AN EXAMPLE OF A CHRIST-CENTERED TRUST LIST IN CONJUNCTION WITH THE BIG QUESTIONS

"In essentials, unity; in non-essentials, liberty; in all things charity."

Augustine of Hippo

In this scene you will find an example of how one might start approaching the Trust List concept when incorporating Christ as the fullness of Reality. This not meant to be an exhaustive list, nor is it meant to be a doctrinal statement or theological treatise. It is simply a sample of how one might begin to approach these big questions with Jesus in mind.

1. What is the nature of Reality? What is really Real?

Christ-centered theists trust that the spiritual and the material are both real. Yet, the spiritual and the material are independent and interdependent with each other as embodied in the Trinity and made manifest in the person of Jesus, who is the fullness of the Father, and the Oneness of the Holy Spirit.

The spiritual realm and material realm are both independently real, yet they coexist and interact independently, interdependently with, and intradependently within each other in various, forms, degrees, and ways. The spiritual and the material realms are fully balanced and made perfect in the Trinity.

2. Who or what is God?

Christ-centered theists trust that God is the all-powerful Creator, the sustainer and the giver of all of life. God is perfect and essentially good in nature and being. God is personal and has personality. God has full authority. God is the standard for and author of morality. Christ-centered theists trust that Jesus truly is God the Father and God the Holy Spirit manifested and incarnate in the body and living being of a man; he is "The Man," the True Human. Jesus as God incarnate walked the streets of the Middle East two thousand years ago as a living, real human being.

3. **Who is Man? What is Mankind? What is a human being? (Who am I? What am I?)**

Christ-centered theists trust that humans are a distinct, wonderful creation made in the image of God, but humans do not possess the exact nature of God nor exist as an extension or part of God. Humans have an individual spirit that is not God's spirit. Jesus is fully man, and He is the True Human who is sinless. He is God the Father and God the Holy Spirit incarnate.

Christ-centered theists trust that the Holy Spirit of God can indwell humans without each human losing his or her identity as independent from God. Yet, they can simultaneously find unity with each other and with God through the one Holy Spirit of God indwelling each individual. With this unique indwelling of God's Holy Spirit, a human can achieve life eternally and individual life to the full as complete and perfected in one's true identity as beloved by God.

4. What is the basis of and standard for morality. How do I decide between right and wrong, and where is the basis for moral authority?

Christ-centered theists trust that all ethical morality is objective based on the personal, all-powerful nature of God who is perfect, loving, and good. God's nature and God's Word, past and present, are the standard for and author of morality. Morality is based on the person, words, and actions of Jesus Christ. A Christ-centered theist leads their life with love; Christ's love is the embodiment and standard for morality. A Christ-centered theist will make Christ's love the primary standard for human interaction, especially concerning morality.

5. What happens to a human at death?

Christ-centered theists trust that when humans die, we have received individual perfection and justification through divine grace and exist eternally in continual relationship with the perfect, personal, loving God. Or, those who have rejected salvation through grace remain in an imperfect, incomplete state and necessarily exist separated from God. When we die, we actualize our True self and exist with God, or we remain eternally separated from perfection and wholeness.

6. What is the meaning and purpose of human history? What is the essence of human interaction and relationships?

Christ-centered theists trust that history is a "linear, meaningful sequence of events leading to the fulfillment of God's purposes for man" in an open system[1]. History is the true, epic, adventure story of God's interaction with mankind, and humans are living within this story. In Essence the book of acts had no "the end" as chapter twenty eight concluded; humans living in this century are a continuation of that story. Humans are independent, autonomous, and gregarious, possessing will and identity as self in communion with others. Jesus' death on the cross and resurrection are the eucatastrophe and centrality of all of human history.

7. Why are we here? Where are we going? What is the purpose of human existence?(To be or not to be? What is the purpose of living for tomorrow?)

Christ-centered theists trust that at least one reason humans exist is to enjoy and experience a meaningful, personal relationship with the Creator and sustainer of life, as reference in act four of this text. We exist in order to expand, enjoy, and protect God's Kingdom through Grace, Truth, and the Power of God's Holy Spirit. We exist so we can bring joy and honor to God and self through genuine worship of God, through loving healthy relationships with God and others, and through authentic serving of God and others.

I end this scene with one of my favorite, and for the content of this text, one of the most poignant quotes from C.S. Lewis[2]. I place it here because of the potent implications of inviting Jesus into your philosophical house and adding this living Being, who happens to be the Creator and sustainer of your soul and the universe, to your personal trust list.

"Imagine yourself as a living house. God comes in to rebuild that house. At first, perhaps, you can understand what He is doing. He is getting the drains right and stopping the leaks in the roof and so on; you knew that those jobs needed doing and so you are not surprised. But presently He starts knocking the house about in a way that hurts abominably and does not seem to make any sense. What on earth is He up to? The explanation is that He is building quite a different house from the one you thought of - throwing out a new wing here, putting on an extra floor there, running up towers, making courtyards. You thought you were being made into a decent little cottage: but He is building a palace. He intends to come and live in it Himself."

C.S. Lewis
Mere Christianity

ACT V, SCENE 4

SOME COST-BENEFIT CONSIDERATIONS FOR CONVERSATIONS ON THE TRUST LISTS.

The following scene is a list that is simply meant to get some more conversations started. It is not exhaustive, and it is organic. Please feel free to disagree, debate, dialogue, discuss, and differentiate. This type of information is helpful when you are trying to figure out what you believe or to start the journey of understanding why someone else might have a different answer on his or her trust list then the one on yours.

Everybody trusts something. Of course, there is a cost to that choice, but of course there are benefits as well—otherwise no human would trust it. In our conversation with people of different worldviews, many people see only the negatives of the other side. It can be invaluable to look for the benefits in other options and trust lists as you assess your own. As this scene unfolds, I have worked hard to try to accurately represent these perspectives with dignity and honor for those who embrace them.

1. What is the nature of Reality? What is really Real?

Idealist

A pure idealist only trusts that the spiritual is really real and that Reality is a state of eternal, spiritual perfection. The material realm is an imperfect, broken, twisted, warped, incomplete shadowy replica of the Ideal: the absolutely good, the perfectly beautiful, and purely true.

> **Cost**: Individual humans do not currently exist physically. Any existence we might posit is in the form of potential, striving, or surrender.

> **Benefit**: The pain, suffering, and chaos of this world makes sense in light of a perfect world that exists independent of this messed up, broken one.

Materialist

An authentic materialist only trusts that the material (the natural) is really real. There is no spiritual realm matter and electricity has existed eternally in various forms and states without beginning or end. That which is observable and measurable is really real. The spiritual realm is a chemical, electrical figment of the human imagination. The spiritual represents all we have yet to figure out how to measure and understand.

Cost: "All we are is all we are…" (Kurt Cobain) Only what is physically measurable is real.

Benefit: We can ultimately measure, define, and predict reality.

Monist

A complete monist trusts that the spiritual and the material are both real, existing as one entity.

The spiritual realm and material realm both exist but are one and the same; there is no true, real separation or distinction. Reality presents itself as dual in nature through polarity and perspectives; however, all of existence is ultimately one, universal, interconnected unity unfolding in various forms.

Cost: You are not an independent human being; there is no real concept of self. All is awareness of self as a piece of god.

Benefit: You are and have always been eternal, and you are connected to everything called god. You have unlimited potential as god.

Theist

A sincere theist trusts that the spiritual and the material are both real, yet independent and interdependent with each other.

The spiritual realm and material realm are both independently real, yet they coexist and interact independently, interdependently with, and intradependently within each other in various, forms, degrees, and ways.

> **Cost:** You are not a part of God; you are a limited creation of God.

> **Benefit:** You have eternal, independent existence as a self. The pain and chaos and joy and beauty of this world makes sense in light of a perfect world that also exists alongside of this one.

Christ-Centered Theist

Christ-centered theists trust that the spiritual and the material are both real, yet independent and interdependent with each other as embodied in the Trinity and made manifest in the person of Jesus, the fullness of the Father, and the oneness of the Holy Spirit. The spiritual realm and the material realm are both independently real, yet they coexist and interact independently, interdependently with, and intradependently within each other in various, forms, degrees, and in various ways. The spiritual and the material are fully balanced and made perfect in the Trinity.

Cost: You are not a part of god; you are a limited creation of God. You are not Jesus, but you are called to be an imitator of Him.

Benefit: You have eternal, independent existence as a self. The pain and chaos and joy and beauty of this world makes sense in light of a perfect world that also exists alongside of this one. Jesus represents pure spirituality and pure material reality in His human and divine nature. Jesus is literally and archetypally the fullness of reality.

2. Who or what is God?

Idealist

A pure idealist trusts that the impersonal, eternal, perfect, one Ideal is what people call god. It is absolute, complete. truth, beauty, and goodness. God is a state of mind and a state of existence. God is the Ideal One that is perfect absolutely and forever. God is the Ideal state of being that is the pursuit of humanity.

Cost:. God is not a being with whom a person can be in a relationship. The perfect cannot be known by the imperfect in our current state of disintegration.

Benefit: The physical brokenness, chaos, suffering, and pain of the world makes sense in light of our search for the Ideal that has yet to be understood by us in our current material state.

Materialist

An authentic materialist trusts that the individual human is his or her own god. There is no creator God. The general definition and attributes of god either disappear as unreal ideas or they fortunately transfer to humanity. There is no objective, powerful being outside of the material. God is a lovely or ugly lie, a figment of man's creativity and imagination, a generative creative idea or concept.

Cost: There is no all-powerful, perfect, objective being who bestows morality, eternal identity, and objective meaning onto our existence. Undeniable, unexplainable, and unpredictable supernatural phenomena causes tension.

Benefit: There is no perfect god out there, no perfect at all. You are already god and you make up your own concept of perfect. There is no objective, all-powerful, spiritual authority to hold you ultimately accountable for your actions or thoughts. In other words, there is no hell and no punishment by god now or after death.

Monist

A complete monist trusts that everything is god. Everything and everybody in the universe is an integral, interconnected part of the unity of life called god.

Existence and reality are what people often call god. The cosmos is filled with duality and polarity as manifested in all of life. Thus, god has a dual nature in essence and being. An undeniable, unexplainable, and unpredictable supernatural phenomenon causes excitement and hope for you to achieve, as well as to worship, the part, or "side" of god you prefer. Often monists worship the deity as a whole as god, the life-force, or mother.

> **Cost:** There is no all-powerful, perfect, objective being who bestows morality, eternal identity, and objective meaning onto our existence.

> **Benefit:** You are already perfect; you already are god. As god, you have unlimited potential. Nothing is impossible for you.

Theist

A sincere theist trusts that there is a God that is the all-powerful Creator, the sustainer and the giver of all life. God is perfect and essentially good in nature and being. God is personal and has personality. God has full authority. God is the standard for and author of morality.

> **Cost:** You are not god, nor will you ever be god. You are an imperfect version of yourself. By necessity, you are unable to be in the presence of the perfect God, who by implication of having a perfect nature, has perfect standards for relationships.

> **Benefit:** There is an all-powerful, perfect, objective being who bestows morality, eternal identity, and objective meaning onto our existence. Undeniable, unexplainable, and unpredictable supernatural phenomena does not need to cause negative tension.

> God is personal and loving and desires to dwell with the perfect version of you now and forever.

Christ-Centered Theist

Christ-centered theists trust that God is the all-powerful Creator, the sustainer, and the giver of all of life. God is perfect and essentially good in nature and being. God is personal and has personality. God has full authority. God is the standard for and author of morality. Christ-centered theists trust that Jesus truly is God the Father and God the Holy Spirit manifested and incarnate in the body and living being of a man. Jesus as God incarnate walked the streets of the Middle East around two thousand years ago as a living, real human being.

Cost: You are not god, nor will you ever be god. You are an imperfect version of yourself. By necessity, you are separated from the presence of the perfect God, who by implication of having a perfect nature, has perfect standards for relationships.

Benefit: There is an all-powerful, perfect, objective being who bestows morality, eternal identity, and objective meaning onto our existence. He has visited our planet and was born in a manger two thousand years ago. This God-man stepped onto our planet and is knowable in the person of Christ. The person of Christ is a human model and an example of divine love and compassion. The person of Jesus offers grace as a means of salvation, as the means to being perfected and made complete so as to dwell with God. The undeniable, unexplainable, and unpredictable, supernatural phenomena does not need to cause negative tension.

3. Who is man? What is mankind? What is a human being?

Idealist

A pure idealist trusts that humans are not perfect. We are one of the infinite, incomplete shadows of the real state of spiritual perfection. Humans exist simply as potential to literally become one with the Ideal. and finally exist as the perfected Ideal in a state of eternal, spiritual perfection and completeness.

> **Cost:** You are simply one of the infinite, imperfect, broken images of the perfect existence that truly exists. In other words, you are an imperfect image of the perfect being.

> **Benefit:** This explains our brokenness and pain and the tensions of this chaotic world. You can become the perfect being—god, or the one—and escape your nonexistence by attaining perfection as god. Once this is achieved, you would then exist eternally as the perfect one.

Materialist

An authentic materialist trusts that human beings are a fascinating, unique, and highly complex system of matter and electricity that is beautifully aware of self and others. Mankind is currently the pinnacle of existence in an infinitely intricate system of cause and effect. Mankind is the amazing realization of the potential and ongoing potential of matter and electricity.

Cost: You exist as long as your body lasts and as long as you are aware of your existence. When life is done, you are done.

You have no free will. You make no real choices. Your life is reduced to cause and effect. You are simply a complex chemical reaction to your environment and various stimuli. Just as a computer has no free will or ability to make independent choices, you are not free either.

Benefit: Life is relatively predictable and measurable, and pain and suffering are explainable in scientific and medical terms. When life is done, you are done. If you reproduce, you have the opportunity to pass on your genes to the future generations.

Monist

A complete monist trusts that a human is a unique, unrepeatable part and parcel of god; we are part of the body of the universe and the entirety of reality appropriately referred to as god. Man is not truly distinct and separate from god, but humans exist as part of reality and the cosmos which, in essence, is part of the entire being of god.

> **Cost:** You are not an independent human being. There is no real concept of self; all awareness of self is as a piece of god. You have to convince yourself that all your thoughts and everybody else's thoughts and actions are part of god.

> **Benefit:** You are and have always been eternal, and you are connected to everything called god. You have unlimited potential as god, and you are a unique unrepeatable part of god.

Theist

A complete theist trusts that humans are a distinct, wonderful creation made in the image of God, but they do not possess the exact nature of God nor do they exist as an extension or part of God.

> **Cost:** You are not a part of God. You are a limited creation of God. You are an imperfect, broken, free being who has fallen from perfection and exists separated from God.

> **Benefit:** You have eternal, independent existence as a self. The pain and chaos and joy and beauty of this world makes sense in light of God's perfect standards. You are

an imperfect, broken, yet free being who has fallen from perfection, but who can choose to attain perfection or acquire perfection from God.

Christ-Centered Theist

Christ-centered theists trust that humans are a distinct, wonderful creation made in the image of God, but they do not possess the exact nature of God nor exist as an extension or part of God. Humans possess an individual spirit that is not God's spirit. Christ-centered theists trust that the Holy Spirit of God can indwell humans without each human losing his or her identity as separate from God. Yet, people can simultaneously find unity with each other and with God through the one Holy Spirit of God indwelling each individual. With this unique indwelling of God's Holy Spirit, a humans can achieve life eternally and individual life to the full as complete and perfected in one's true identity as beloved by God.

Cost: You are not a part of God; you are a limited creation of God. You are an imperfect, broken, free being who has fallen from perfection and exists separated from God.

Benefit: You will have eternal, independent existence as a self. The pain and chaos and joy and beauty of this world makes sense in light of God's perfect standards You are an imperfect, broken, yet free being who has fallen from perfection but can choose to attain, acquire, and sustain perfection and wholeness from God through the redemptive work of Christ's death on the cross and resurrection from the dead. Humans can live with the mystery of the gospel, which is Christ indwelling you.

4. What is the basis of and standard for morality? How do I decide between right and wrong, and where is the basis for moral authority?

Idealist

A pure idealist trusts that all morality is objective based on the nature of the impersonal, perfect Spiritual Ideal, which is absolute truth, perfect beauty, and complete goodness. All thought and behavior is completely aimed at achieving and sustaining this state of existence.

> **Cost:** You do not get to decide what is right and wrong based on your personal preference.

> **Benefit:** Good and evil in this world makes sense based on the objective nature of the perfect, good, and true standard for behavior, the ideal One. Right and wrong behavior is definable, comprehensible, and achievable.

Materialist

An authentic materialist trusts that all morality is ultimately subjective and based on self, majority, and/or power. Morality is essentially absurd at the core.

There is no truly objective standard for good and evil for humans, nor can there ever be. Therefore, all morality is relative, based on value and agreed submission (or rejection) to a constructed system of human authority, community, and power.

> **Cost:** Objective, ultimate morality is absurd. Good and evil, right and wrong behavior, are subject to personal preference, power, or majority. Morality is reduced to cause and effect in a closed system.

> **Benefit:** If you can make the electrical, material system of existence work for your personal benefit, you can do anything you like, guilt free. If you can avoid or change negative, natural, cause-and-effect consequences, you can do whatever you want. There are no personal, postmortem consequences for any of your actions or thoughts.

Monist

A complete monist trusts that morality is completely subjective based 'souly' on one's individual preference as a part of the interconnected universal reality called god. God's morality as manifested in the universe is dual in nature. God consists of positive and negative energy, creative and destructive forces, darkness and light, heat and cold, et cetera, ad infinitum.

> **Cost:** Objective, ultimate morality is absurd. Good and evil do not exist except as descriptive words. Right and wrong behavior is subject to personal preference. Because everyone is part of god, morality is reduced to a description of whatever happens as part of the infinite impulses and expressions of the existence of god. Evil and bad behavior do not exist, because all behavior is a part of god.

> **Benefit:** *I am intentionally replicating these responses because they fit in both categories depending on your perspective and preference as a monist.* Objective, ultimate morality is absurd. Good and evil do not exist except as descriptive words. Right and wrong behavior is open to personal preference because everyone is part of god. Morality is elevated to a description of whatever happens as part of the infinite impulses and expressions of the existence of god. Evil

and bad behavior do not exist because all behavior is a part of god often in the form of tribal or shaman morality.

Theist

A sincere theist trusts that all ethical morality is objective based on the personal, all-powerful nature of God who is perfect and good. God, God's word, and God's nature are the standard for and author of morality. While this may include ritual traditions or cultural norms, it does not necessarily have to.

> **Cost:** You do not get to decide what is right and wrong based on your personal preference

> **Benefit:** Good and evil in this world makes sense, because they are based on the objective nature of the perfect, good, true, loving, and personal God. Right and wrong behavior is definable, comprehensible, and achievable.

Christ-Centered Theist

Christ-centered theists trust that all ethical morality is objective based on the personal, all-powerful nature of God who is perfect, loving, and good. God's nature and God's word, past and present, are the standard for and author of morality. Morality is based on the person, words, and actions of Jesus Christ. A Christ-centered theist is motivated by love; Christ's love is the standard for morality. Love, based on the person of

Christ, becomes the primary standard for human interaction, especially concerning morality.

Cost: You do not get to decide what is right and wrong based on your personal preference.

Benefit: Good and evil in this world makes sense, because they are based on the objective nature of the perfect, good, true, loving, and personal God and on the life, words, and actions of Jesus. Right and wrong behavior is definable, comprehensible, and explainable in the context of the behavior and attitudes of Christ. Religion and morality regain a new context embedded in the love of Christ. Love is the new standard of morality, and believers in Christ are empowered and gifted by His Spirit to live and love as His beloved disciples.

5. What happens to a human at death?

Idealist

A pure idealist trusts that when we die, perfection is attained and oneness with the Ideal is achieved. We realize our potential, we let go of the imperfect representation of self, and become one with the state of spiritual perfection. A pure idealist might also say we cease to exist as an imperfect self and shadowy, broken representation of perfection. We simply cease to exist materially on Earth; individually, we cease to exist.

Cost: You truly cease to exist. You now lose awareness as an imperfect shadow, because you did not achieve perfection and unity with the perfect one.

Benefit: You cease to exist as an imperfect shadow. Because you did relinquish your prior identity and you have achieved perfection and unity with the perfect one, you literally become god by becoming one with god. You are now one with the ideal, perfect one. Or, in some religions, you get another chance to attain perfection via reincarnation..

You either cease to exist because you become god, or you cease to exist because you are not perfect.

Materialist

An authentic materialist trusts that humans cease to be aware of one's existence at the point of death. There is no eternal existence of one's spiritual soul beyond the grave, because there is no eternal, spiritual soul dwelling in the human body.

Cost: If your existence is pleasurable, it is over when you die. You cease to exist and your awareness stops. There is no eternal life awareness or existence as god or with a . personal god.

Benefit: If your existence is miserable, it is over when you die. You cease to exist and your awareness stops. There is no life awareness of eternal separation from a loving and personal god. There is no hell. There are no negative eternal consequences for not being perfect.

Monist

A complete monist trusts that when a human dies, we morph into another part of existence and another component of reality, which is god. The shared, united soul shifts into another part of the cosmos with another unique perspective on living as god.

Cost: If your existence is pleasurable, it is over when you die. You cease to exist as your current part of god. There is no eternal life as yourself with an objective, personal, loving, relational god.

Benefit: Death does not exist. Death is simply a transformation into another opportunity to exist as another part of god perpetually.

Theist

A sincere theist trusts that when humans die, we obtain individual perfection and exist eternally in continual relationship with the perfect, personal God or we remain in an imperfect, incomplete state and necessarily exist separated from God.

When we die, we actualize our true self and exist with God, or we are eternally separated from perfection and wholeness.

> **Cost:** The possibility of continual awareness of a real separation from the loving and perfect, relational God.

> **Benefit:** You get to dwell with the perfect, loving, and good God as your actualized, perfect version of yourself.

Depending on your version of religion and the unique denomination of that religion which pulls from these core philosophical principles, you either:

> A) Personally attain perfection of self and thus gain the right to dwell with God by making yourself worthy of existence with the perfect God.

> B) Behave well enough to please the perfect God, and then the perfect God chooses to clean up or to overlook your imperfections so you can exist with the perfect God.

> C) In order to allow imperfect humans dwell with their perfect Creator, the perfect God simply makes all of His creation perfect, whether they want this or not.

> D) You follow the perfect God's system of sacrifice and

atonement to perfectly cleanse yourself of all of your imperfection so that you can dwell with the perfect God.

E) You acknowledge that as an imperfect version of yourself, you cannot fully please God nor can you attain perfection on your own. So, you simply ask and trust the perfect God to make you the perfect version of yourself so that you can dwell with the perfect God.

Christ-Centered Theist

Christ-centered theists trust that when humans die, we have received individual perfection and justification through divine grace. As such, we exist eternally in continual relationship with the perfect personal loving God, or we remain in an imperfect, incomplete state having rejected salvation through divine grace and exist separated from God.

When we die, we actualize our true self and exist with God, or we remain eternally separated from perfection and wholeness.

Cost: The possibility of continual awareness of a real and eternal separation from the loving and perfect relational God

Benefit: You get to dwell with the perfect, loving, and good God as your actualized, perfected version of yourself.

6. What is the meaning and purpose of human history? What is the essence of human interaction and relationships?

Idealist

A pure idealist trusts that history and memory are a record of humans striving to escape nonexistence and attain an ideal state of spiritual perfection. Human interaction is summed up and actualized in striving to escape nonexistence alone or together.

> **Cost:** History is full of a shadows suffering and striving to become real.

> **Benefit:** You can learn what not to do and try to imitate the few who made it.

Materialist

An authentic materialist trusts that humans, individually or collectively, get to create our own meaning for existence. History and memory are ultimately absurd with no objective overarching meaning or purpose.

History is a story of a linear sequence of events and phenomena linked by cause and effect in a closed system (such as natural selection). Human interaction is literally chemistry and pure cause and effect.

Cost: There is no meaning. Events happen and unfold in a closed system; history is absurd, simply chemical images of the past. Tensions arise from the inexplicable or the absurdity of chance defining our lives.

Benefit: You can learn from cause and effect in a closed system. History is open for interpretation, and history is absurd.

Monist

A complete monist trusts that history and memory consist of the repository of collective memories of our collective coexistence as god. In other words, humans are connected to history as part of the unfolding story of the cosmos which is god.

Cost: You are literally a part of history and can connect with your own past.

Benefit: You are literally a part of history and can connect with your own past.

Theist

A sincere theist trusts that history is a "linear, meaningful sequence of events leading to the fulfillment of God's purposes for man" in an open system[1]. History is the true, epic, adventure story of God's interaction with mankind. Humans are independent, autonomous, and gregarious, possessing will and identity as self in communion with others.

> **Cost:** You and I are not in control of interpreting the past for our own personal agendas.

> **Benefit:** God is the author and focus of history, and it is a story God is writing and has already written.

Christ-Centered Theist

Christ-centered theists trust that history is a "linear, meaningful sequence of events leading to the fulfillment of God's purposes for man" in an open system[1]. History is the true, epic, adventure story of God's interaction with mankind that we are currently participating in. Humans are independent, autonomous, and gregarious, possessing will and identity as self in communion with others. Jesus' death on the cross and resurrection are the eucatastrophe and centrality of all of human history.

> **Cost:** You and I are not in control of interpreting the past for our personal agendas.

> **Benefit:** God is the author and focus of history, and it is a story that God is writing and has already written. Christ's birth, ministry, death, and resurrection are the

center of all history.

7. Why are we here? Where are we going? What is the purpose of human existence? (To be or not to be? What is the purpose of living for tomorrow?)

Idealist

A pure idealist trusts that we exist only to achieve and sustain an ideal state spiritual perfection, to escape painful non-existence, and to exist eternally through becoming one with the Ideal One by existing eternally as absolutely perfectly good, beautiful, and true in and as the Spiritual Ideal.

> **Cost:** Life is continual striving and suffering in painful awareness of nonexistence, ending in nothingness. You are going nowhere.

> **Benefit:** One can achieve perfection and escape suffering as a shadow and can eventually exist eternally as perfection. You get to be god, eventually.

Materialist

An authentic materialist trusts that we get to create our own meaning for life. However, at the core, life is essentially, objectively absurd because there is no objective meaning or purpose, nor can there be. Humans can live for whatever brings pleasure or the hope of pleasure.

We can hope for or create beneficial change of circumstances with the goal of increasing positive and decreasing negative natural consequences.

> **Cost:** Life is completely, unabashedly absurd and void of any objective meaning. Everybody else can also do whatever they desire if they can avoid personal negative consequences. Pain, suffering, and trauma are pointless and absurd. Life is over when it is over or when you cease to be aware of your own existence.

> **Benefit:** Life is completely, unabashedly absurd and void of any objective meaning. Have a blast and do whatever you like. Avoid negative personal consequences, live guilt free, and create your own meaning. Life is over when it is over or when you cease to be aware of your own existence.

Monist

A complete monist trusts that every human has the exciting opportunity to continue experiencing being various components of universal reality—of god—forever. We are here to wake up to who we are as a unique part of god and reach our full potential as our part of the divine existence and unity of god.

Cost: Life is completely, unabashedly absurd and void of any objective meaning. Everybody else can also do whatever they desire as god, and they can use the state of being god as reason for their behavior. Pain, suffering, and trauma are part of god and thus not bad or evil; they just are. There is no good and evil or right and wrong.

Benefit: Life is completely, unabashedly hopeful and yet void of any objective meaning Have a blast and do whatever you like. Embrace you current status as god and embrace all experiences in life as god. Live guilt free and create your own meaning. Life is never over. You can do whatever you want. You are god, and everything is personal preference. Enjoy your existence devoid of good and evil. Just exist.

Theist

A sincere theist trusts that at least one reason humans exist is to enjoy and experience a meaningful, personal relationship with the Creator and sustainer of life. We exist in order to expand, enjoy, and protect God's Kingdom.

We exist so we can bring joy and honor to God and self through genuine worship of God, loving, healthy relationships with God and others, and through authentic serving of God and others.

>   **Cost:** You do not get to create your own meaning. If a person chooses not to be in a personal relationship with God, or if a person chooses not to submit to God as the ultimate authority on morality, there are severe, negative, natural, and supernatural consequences

>   **Benefit:** You exist to do what you were created to do: love God and love others. If you choose to submit to God's authority and plan for your existence, you can receive personal self-actualization, joy, and existence in a meaningful, personal relationship with your Creator. Meaning is defined by God. You have eternal purpose and meaning given to you by a loving, all-powerful, personal, perfect, objective God.

Christ-Centered Theist

Christ-centered theists trust that at least one reason humans exist is to enjoy and experience a meaningful, personal relationship with the Creator and sustainer of life. We exist in order to expand, enjoy, and protect God's kingdom through grace, truth, and the power of God's Holy Spirit. We exist so we can bring joy and honor to God and self through genuine worship of God, through loving, healthy relationships with God and others, and through authentic serving of God and others.

Cost: Meaning is defined by God. You do not get to create your own meaning.

Benefit: Meaning is defined in relationship with God. You exist to fulfill God's eternal purpose and plan for your life as intentionally created beings who are designed by Him to fill the earth with the glory of His reflection through the power of His Spirit.

Reflection

1. What ideas or images stood out to you in this chapter?

2. What was refreshing? Why?

3. What was frustrating? Why?

4. What questions do you have?

ACT V, SCENE 5

THE ROAD GOES EVER ON

"The Road goes ever on and on
Down from the door where it began.
Now far ahead the Road has gone,
And I must follow, if I can,
Pursuing it with weary feet,
Until it joins some larger way,
Where many paths and errands meet.
And wither then? I cannot say."

J.R.R. Tolkien
Frodo, *Fellowship of the Ring*

Many blessings to you on your quest for the Truth. I hope that the pages in this text have been helpful on your journey. I hope that you will continue to build a strong trust list to guide you through the choices of each day here on Faith Island. Like all great adventures, I trust that you will have, or have already had, or are having perilous moments. Richard Rhor, in his challenging book *Falling Upward*[2], echoes Jesus's words down through the centuries when he pointedly says,

"You must die before you die." This journey of trust can be a pain-filled journey at times. Often it takes all the courage we can muster simply to make it through the next moment and to take the next step.

Fortunately, the best epic adventures and the best stories have the greatest triumphs and treasures as well. These triumphs and treasures are the marrow of life and the substance of each day that makes life worth living. They give us hope and a desire for eternal life with the Truth Himself. I risk being trite offering this as a final sentiment. Nevertheless, the great fairy tales tell us about the hope and potential for this unfolding tale we find ourselves in. So many of them end with, "and they lived happily ever after." I firmly believe that the Truth will set us free—free to fully live, both now and forevermore. I leave you with two quotes to ponder as you put down this text, one from J.R.R. Tolkien and one from the prophet Isaiah.

From Sam, right in the middle of his challenging adventure with Frodo in *The Lord of the Rings*: "It's like in the great stories, Mr. Frodo. The ones that really mattered. Full of darkness and danger they were. And sometimes you didn't want to know the end... because how could the end be happy? How could the world go back to the way it was when so much bad had happened? But in the end, it's only a passing thing... this shadow. Even darkness must pass."

J.R.R. Tolkien
The Two Towers

You shall go out in joy and be led forth in peace; the mountains and hills will burst into song before you, and all the trees of the field will clap their hands.

Isaiah 55:12 (NIV)

Endnotes

Introduction

1. Tolkien, J.R.R. "On Fairy Stories." *Leaf and Tree*. Boston: Houghton-Mifflin, 1965.
2. Lewis, C.S. "Myth Became Fact." *C.S. Lewis Essay Collection: Faith, Christianity, and the Church*. Ed. Lesley Walmsley. London: HarperCollins, 2002.

Act I, Scene 2

1. Brown, Willliam. "World of Worldview." *The Torch*. Cedarville University, 2004.

Act I, Scene 3
1. Chesterton, G.K. *Orthodoxy*. Wheaton: Harold Shaw Publishers, 1994.

Act I, Scene 4
1. Chesterton, G.K. *Orthodoxy*. Wheaton: Harold Shaw Publishers, 1994.

Act II, Scene 1
1. Chesterton, G.K. *Collected Works*. San Francisco: Ignatius Press, 1986.

Act II, Scene 2
1. *Oxford English Dictionary*. New York: Oxford University Press, 1989.
2. "axiom." *Merriam-Webster.com*. 2015. Web.
3. "perfection." *Merriam-Webster.com*. 2015. Web.

Act II, Scene 3
1. Penninga, Mike. "God, I Have a Question...Part 2 Don't All Roads Lead to You?" *Kelowna Gospel Fellowship Church*. April 2013. Web. www.kgfchurch.com

Act III, Scene 1
1. Sire, James. *Universe Next Door*. Downers Grove: InterVarsity Press, 2009.

Act III, Scene 5
1. Sire, James. *Universe Next Door*. Downers Grove: InterVarsity Press, 2009.

Act IV
1. Chesterton, G.K. *Orthodoxy*. Wheaton: Harold Shaw Publishers, 1994.

Act IV, Scene 1
1. Lewis, C.S. *The Weight of Glory*. New York: HarperCollins, 2001.

Act IV, Scene 2
1. Chesterton, G.K. *Orthodoxy*. Wheaton: Harold Shaw Publishers, 1994.

Act V
1. Tolkien. J.R.R.. *The Fellowship of the Ring*. Boston: Houghton-Mifflin, 2002.

Act V, Scene 2
1. Lewis. C.S.. *Mere Christianity*. New York: Touchstone, 1996.

Act V, Scene 3
1. Sire, James. *Universe Next Door*. Downers Grove: InterVarsity Press, 2009.
2. Lewis. C.S.. *Mere Christianity*. New York: Touchstone, 1996.

Act V, Scene 4
1. Sire, James. *Universe Next Door*. Downers Grove: InterVarsity Press, 2009.

Act V, Scene 5
1. Tolkien. J.R.R.. *The Fellowship of the Ring*. Boston: Houghton-Mifflin, 2002.
2. Rohr, Richard. *Falling Upward*. San Francisco: Jossey-Bass, 2011.
3. Tolkien. J.R.R.. *The Two Towers*. Boston: Houghton-Mifflin, 2002.